THE JAPANESE

CULT OF TRANQUILLITY

KARLFRIED GRAF VON
DÜRCKHEIM

THE JAPANESE CULT
OF TRANQUILLITY

SAMUEL WEISER INC.
New York

SAMUEL WEISER INC.
734 Broadway, New York 10003

First published 1960
This United States edition 1974

Printed in Great Britain
ISBN 0-87728-244-7

Contents

I

Tranquillity in the East and the West

Man's inborn knowledge of tranquillity

THE age into which we are born is fundamentally opposed to tranquillity and every decade increases the antagonism between the two. The present time would therefore seem to be the very antithesis of a cult of tranquillity. Yet perhaps at no time more than today are men so filled with longing for stillness, and so ready to yield themselves to it, if they could only know where to find it.

The reverberations of our own technical world deafen us, while our sensitivity to noise is heightened by restricted space and time; few can escape the harsh sound of voices trying to drown each other, surely a most forcible expression of the inner and outer distress in every sphere of life. Nowadays stillness is only to be experienced for most in the silence of death, of ruined buildings, of resignation. Behind it all lurks an awareness of total destruction. Millions of men and women seem paralysed at the annihilation of everything that once gave purpose to their lives. They are hypnotized by destructive forces obliterating the past and undermining the future, and they are powerless to break the spell.

However, the very omnipresence of these destructive powers, which threaten man from without and poison him from within, arouses a natural desire for what is indestructible, in so far as his nature itself is still unharmed. Similarly his sensitivity to noise arouses a desire for tranquillity such as reflects an accomplished life, and not the silence of death. In actual fact both are aiming at the same thing; a desire for what is indestructible and a desire for the blessing of true tranquillity.

Yet our power to perceive tranquillity seems to be muted or non-existent! Is it not so that man today no longer possesses the ability, the will, nor even the courage, which are its necessary requisites? Would it not be true to say that he is afraid of it, as though stillness were a terrifying void and at the sight of it man is seized with horror, the *horror vacui*, as always when life reveals its true depth to him for a brief moment?

Where man loses touch with the kernel of his essential being, he identifies himself exclusively with his outer shell. When his sense of inner achievement becomes muted, he turns to the clamour of the world without and, losing all sense of the living centre, is caught in the bondage of a hardened periphery. Alienated from his spiritual powers, man tries to find fulfilment in protecting and indulging his own ego, in the excitement of cheap stimuli, or the satisfaction of his instinctive desires, or even in the sensations of a disproportionate mind, whose very roots are withered. Man becomes a refuge from himself. He takes flight from life's calm rhythm to find refuge in the measured beat of organized existence, relinquishing his contact with the indestructible within himself for security in the transitory world, and drowning the quiet voices of being in the clamour of worthless illusion.

Man is all too prone to justify his denial of the true substance of his existence on the plea of the external exigencies of life. But can he do so with a clear conscience?

Are there not sufficient occasions in every human life when true tranquillity beckons him and ultimate reality appeals to him in its own voice?

Deep in the heart of man there exists a hidden knowledge that true tranquillity such as the soul desires is something more than a mere beneficial lack of noise, more than the mere counterpoise of rest, as opposed to restlessness and overtaxed strength, that it is even more than the presupposition of spiritual life, or a mere precondition of mental fitness. Man knows that true tranquillity supersedes all this and is not just something that presupposes a happy life: it is the actual experiencing of fulfilment of life. Even our own times have not fully overshadowed the innate experience that when man is genuinely happy he becomes tranquil and, conversely, when he achieves genuine stillness it is only then that he discovers true happiness.

At all times people have experienced the joys of tranquillity and have sought to establish it within themselves. Again and again there have been instances of schools of wisdom whose purpose has been to lead men to tranquillity. The great religions have all been ways towards this end. But men differ in their receptivity of it and in their willingness to sacrifice in order to achieve it. They differ from reasons of age, development, and character. A man who has been tried by life is nearer tranquillity than one who has not gone through the school of suffering. A superficial person is farther from it than one endowed with knowledge of the interior life. The peasant is more familiar with it than a man whom city life has in its thralls; yet he to whom life has denied natural peace is often far more sensitive to its appeal, and consequently to experience of it, than someone who is still part of Nature and enjoys it as a matter of course.

For many different reasons individuals, eras, and

9

nations vary as to their degree of receptivity. The East is more familiar with tranquillity of the mind than the West. The East is more receptive both through natural inclination as well as in consequence of a long tradition of education and practice, which senses a fundamental threat to life in whatever stands in the way of tranquillity.

Whoever has the opportunity of living for some time in the Far East will notice that there men seek and understand tranquillity more than we do, not merely external stillness, but tranquillity as life in its absolute form. For them it is the expression of life's natural harmony, a criterion of all that is worth while in life, and finally as the mark of a life which has achieved perfection. It is the East which recognizes tranquillity as effective reality of primordial character, a reality which man has been destined to recognize and develop, to experience and protect. Therefore, there is an actual cult of tranquillity in existence in the East. This cult is very often at the centre of conscious acts. Thus knowledge of the 'cult of tranquillity' provides also a key to understanding the specifically Japanese mind and it is a rewarding task to undertake. It is rewarding, not only in its being an interesting revelation of Far Eastern thought, but because it concerns ourselves as well. We are here concerned with an original phenomenon of human nature, whose continued existence in the West is in danger of being overshadowed to such an extent by other forces that our innermost human self is imperilled. By looking into the mirror of the East the West will be able to become more conscious of itself, both as to its potentialities and to the dangers which threaten it from within. It will recognize its own individuality and the general human traits which the latter exemplifies; furthermore it will see the inherent dangers in its own overemphasis on particularism, that this might eventually undermine the wholeness of human being which is the living source of all that may be considered 'individual'.

The Japanese cult of tranquillity

Anyone who has paid merely a passing visit to the East, perhaps only to the big cities, will have noticed few traces of a cult of tranquillity. His chief recollection may well be the deafening noise in his ears of a Chinese town, or the shrill sounds of a Chinese theatre. By comparison, the Japanese towns are far quieter. Yet even Japan is a country which has occasionally disturbed Europeans, in that the Japanese is insensitive to noise to an almost inconceivable degree. In trains nobody is distracted by the ceaseless crying of an infant; the mother in the home appears quite unconscious of the rowdy games of the boys, nor does the scholar appear to notice the clamour of children playing about in the same room. At some time or other every visitor at a formal party in a tea-house must have been struck by the small concern of his host, when, just as the evening is beginning in conventional silence in the room set apart for the meal, the paper walls are pierced by the sound of geishas singing to the accompaniment of shamiseu, and even by the uncontrolled laughter of guests in the next room.

This strange imperturbable quality of the Japanese is by no means a lack of sensitivity to noise, but the product of long training. One comes to admire this quality all the more as one gradually realizes that the Japanese apparent insensitivity to noise is the result of his systematic cultivation of certain inner forces. The Japanese owes his admirable ability to preserve inner tranquillity amidst the clamour of life, neither to his being naturally 'thick skinned' nor to any innate phlegmatic character, nor even to an originally harmonious nature, but to spiritual training. This became an inner necessity for him for the very reason that, in comparison with Europeans and even with the Chinese, the Japanese is particularly sensitive, easily hurt, and actually unharmonious in structure. Thus he can be more easily disturbed by external things than they and become a prey to forces within himself which because of his frail temperament might easily shatter his composure. The Japanese therefore protects himself against the outer world by a self-imposed screen which enables him to preserve his tranquillity amid the change and stress of life. This tranquillity, however, which he endeavours to cultivate, means far more than mere freedom from external distraction. The source of deepest self-consciousness, the root of our individual being, which is fundamentally identical with universal being, is at stake. It is not only in order to be able to face the perils of life from within and from without that he learns to cultivate tranquillity, he seeks it for its own sake, as a permanent feature of his self. What he seeks is not so much the natural as the supernatural blessing which it evokes. He is concerned with preserving and cultivating the inner organ which enables us to assimilate what emanates from tranquillity as such and from it alone.

A preference for the simple fundamentals of life characterizes the Japanese and the entire Orient. The Japanese has therefore trained this preference on the basis of his specific physical and psychic disposition in a long tradition of self-discipline. The result is a cult of stillness which everywhere in Japan enchants all who have eyes to perceive it; in the cult of home and garden, in handicrafts and the arts, in conventions and ritual practices, but above all in the peculiar radiance which emanates from the mature.

Tranquillity itself is the object of specific exercises. For a long time past 'exercises in tranquillity' have been the normal practice of everyday life. They find expression in particular customs and popular pursuits and they are a necessary part of the curriculum of various 'arts', which are taught in the master groups. They culminate in the contemplative exercises of Buddhist monks and Shintoist priests, in whose religious exercises they possibly originated. Thus, in Japan every form of life, in as much as it is truly Japanese and not counteracted by the influence of Western civilization, is permeated by exercises in tranquillity. An understanding of this Japanese cult of stillness and of the exercises which lead up to it presupposes a knowledge of the specifically Japanese way of life which has produced it.

The concept of culture in Japan and in the West

In the cultural consciousness of every race we meet with a distinctive attitude of man towards life and death. This attitude varies from one culture to another. To the people living within a specific culture their attitude is, as a matter of course, the only possible one and they presume that it alone is universally valid. Not merely do they look quite unconsciously at other cultures through their own eyes, but judge in perfect naïvety the achievements and the value of other cultures in the light of their own concept. Thus the educated European, who appreciates this difficulty theoretically, still manages to make the naïve mistake of considering the culture of the East to be more primitive than his. He is then not a little surprised to find that the East, according to its conception, considers European culture inferior to its own. Although the East recognizes the superior achievements of Western civilization, it sees in the Western emphasis on rational thought and technical power, which override true human culture, the expression of an immature or even primitive approach to life and death. To Eastern eyes this shows inability to develop beyond a Promethean, illusory attitude which may well befit a young man but which is hardly compatible with maturity.

There are two motive forces which appear to the sensibility of the Far East to have created the body of Western civilization: on the one hand the extravagant instinct to protect and develop human existence here and now, and on the other hand, equally erroneous, the instinct to master life by means of rational explanations and accomplishments. The extent to which the peoples of the West yield to these instincts seems to prove to the East that they have failed to understand the true significance of life. For them our culture is a specifically material civilization, possessing a freedom to dispose of Nature to which man has no right. Our 'cult of the objective mind' temporarily suspends man from the realities of human existence by giving him a share in a world beyond time and space, whenever he is successfully engaged in creating or contemplating 'valid forms'. The Eastern mind sees in the prevalence of this tendency the danger of a major error such as will deprive man of the solemnity, if not the possibilities, of death, which is, after all, an inevitable part of human destiny. Western mentality is characterized by its exaggerated instinct for being 'independent of Nature' and by its pronounced susceptibility for the timeless character of valid forms. Added to this is a particular talent for creating perfect works whose timeless character robs the sphere of temporal existence of its fateful power. Eastern sensibility considers that these propensities endanger the path which man's destiny would have him follow. The Oriental has to smile at the excessive prominence given to the sense of insecurity even among apparently cultured Europeans. He is even more taken aback to see how men of the West are irritated by discrepancies in those patterns of being which his mind has discovered or created in the phenomenal world, and which do not absolutely correspond to his pre-conception of them. He regards our strange struggle against Nature with astonishment and is even more aston-ished (since the East has no Greek heritage) at our striving towards objective form, as the perfect realization of an idea. He terms it 'the Western form disease'. And so he regards the Western world in wonder, and not without a certain reserve, watching its attempts to eliminate such hard-ships as are an implicit part of life by creating remedies which merely add to extant necessities. He sees progress merely driving man into still more extravagant efforts to develop, indulge, and assert himself, ensnaring him in a world of make-believe through an illusory share in the permanency of valid forms; man imagines himself able to transcend natural life and is therefore all the less prepared for intense suffering when he recognizes the inevitability of fate. For fate will only be met in the right way where man is prepared to accept death.

Against a background of Western culture we can clearly appreciate the very different approach to life and death among the peoples of the East. The concept 'life' has a completely different implication; so, too, has death. The prevailing Western concept of death is opposed to that of life, whereas the Eastern concept of life embraces both simultaneously. The meaning of this may be grasped in the image of the relation between the leaf and the tree: if the little leaf on the big tree were conscious of its own indi-viduality, and limited its vital consciousness to being nothing but a leaf, it would feel its life limited to its own life span. Death in autumn would mean the destroying of its life and would be antagonistic to its consciousness of life. It would be therefore hardly surprising if this leaf should attempt to enjoy its short life as a leaf to the utmost, to protect itself against autumn and winter, and forget its fear of death in a dream world of unending leaf-images. Would it not, however, be possible for the little leaf to experience its existence as a leaf in deepened self-consciousness as a mode of the tree's realizing its being as a tree? Would it not be nearer its own 'reality' too, if it identified its own self-consciousness with that of the tree, that is, if it should feel its individual existence to be the form of the tree, whose greater life gives birth to the lesser life of the leaf, surviving it and embracing its death in itself.

The image should not be exaggerated but for the moment it may indicate what we are referring to here—that the prevalent concept of life for the Eastern person is that of the 'Greater Life' which transcends all 'Lesser Life' and the death of the latter, and yet manifests itself in both. And where, in Lesser Life, Greater Life manifests itself not only unconsciously, but also, as in man, becoming aware of itself and conscious of its all-embracing nature, the true significance of culture becomes apparent. Culture consists in revealing the Greater Life in the Lesser, in imitation of the one by the other, and overcoming all natural inclination on the part of the Lesser Life to assert itself absolutely and thus to become opposed to death and the transitory world. To accept this task as a matter of course and to attempt it again and again is only possible for men whose concept of the Greater Life is the result of a constant reunion with the latter and which does not proceed from some edifice in the mind or some metaphysical speculation.

Seen against this background, Western culture appears to be the product of fear of death. Here man is embued with the delusion of having to endure perpetually and falls prey either to his instinct of self-preservation or, still more deadly, to the facile ability of his mind to construct a timeless world of 'values' which conceals the true nature of life from him. In comparison with the Western approach to life, Eastern culture seems to mean mastery of the fear of death, which sucks man back in his efforts to ascend from the prison of his ego-mind towards true Life, which embraces death and the transitory world. The East considers that the essence of life is revealed beyond all doubt in change and that this true substance can only be attained, in a manner in conformity with life, if man follows a way of trans-mutation of himself by returning to himself and ascending anew from there. The meaning of life can therefore only be realized by man if he attains union with life in its totality instead of merely trying to understand and fulfil it object-ively. This union with life in its totality invalidates the opposition of Subject and Object and accepts fate in a fraternal unity of life and death.

The Japanese is as fond of life as we are, cherishing power and property, suffering sickness and death, and possessing a positive appreciation of all life's joys. However, to cling to material possessions, complain over losses, to be dis-tracted at suffering, or become bitter in old age, or to overlook death and try to outwit fate by having a share in an imaginary world beyond time, and to oppose the law of change, is for the Japanese the mark of great im-maturity and therefore of a want of culture. People are cold in winter because it is winter. A bitter old man is a comic figure. As for death, it is part of life. A man who thinks otherwise has little understanding, he is not yet 'on the way' and deserves no pity. There is but one way: the one upon which man humbly fulfils the external law of change thanks to his oneness—whether original or renewed —with the Greater Life which manifests itself in change.

Doubtless men in the West, living and feeling as Christians, possess a concept of life as a whole which

17

embraces the individual life and its death, and is just as far removed from the diabolic instinct for self-preservation as from the presumptions of a mind which asserts itself absolutely against fate and life. But this Christian consciousness which is also to be found in the West is opposed to the forces which have determined the cast of Western civilization and which remain the prevalent forces today. Conversely, the Japanese, because he is a human being like ourselves, is thoroughly aware of the temptations of the ego, and of the intellect, which his cultural instinct demands him to overcome. When confronting the Eastern and the Western 'mind', however, we are not concerned with what is 'also' to be found there or here, but with the prevailing features of both civilizations, and with what determines the inner and outward forms of life on a basis of natural ability, tradition, and education. Even the Christian heritage is moulded by the worldly, active, and creative attitude of man in the West; it is natural that of the two poles of Christian teaching in the West, the one directed towards the work of creation should predominate culturally over the one concerned with the path of salvation. There can be no doubt that the vital instinct of self-preservation dominates man's consciousness in the West, despite all other forces of Christian origin urging a different way. To this is joined a cult of objectivity by which man aspires to overcome human fate through acts of creation. In Japan, on the other hand, despite all antagonistic human talents, impulses, and needs, the predominant cultural instinct, apparent in all fertile creative activity, is determined by the knowledge that Greater Life is superior to death. Such is the nature of this knowledge that it becomes just as impossible for the instinct of self-preservation to triumph at all costs over human consciousness, as it does for objectivity to be made the saviour of human suffering.

This is not the place to mention the reasons for such dissimilarity nor to inquire as to the worth or validity of the civilizations which have sprung from the two concepts. One question in particular must remain open, and that is how far the European is capable of forming a truer union with Greater Life than the Japanese, through the very fact that the European is particularly susceptible to the temptations of his ego and his intellect and forced to experience them on account of his predisposition for 'objective' achievements. The Japanese mistrusts the powers of his ego and the talents of his intellect from the outset. Consequently, his sense of there being a world of ideas and valid forms, such as characterizes the West, is far less developed and is overshadowed by other talents. Western culture is above all a culture of performing 'works'; it sets its intellectual powers and mastery of form against life's vicissitudes, and with mental weapons aspires to safeguard freedom and the dignity of the self-reliant in a world which shall outlast time. Eastern culture, on the other hand, is predominantly one of being on the inner 'way'. In it man accepts existence and its concomitant perils, submitting himself to the law of change which is effective in them, and aspiring towards absolute union with the Oneness of Life which this law makes manifest.

The various approaches to tranquillity

The spiritual outlook of the West accepts reckless conflict with the forces of Nature as readily as it accepts restless mental activity, and man's only acquaintance with the blessings of tranquillity is in moments of passing victory. Yet this hardly won prize is soon snatched from him by renewed concerns for safeguards, or by the instinct to devise still more perfect forms and systems which is the consequence of every achievement. A 'cult of tranquillity' cannot spring from such an attitude, but only a constant craving which cannot be satisfied until man grows wise and, as it were, surrenders himself to it. The very craving for deep tranquillity of soul, at which the instincts for self-security and creative activity subside, may well appear to the people of the West to imply weakness or ineffectual old age. If, however, as in the East, the purpose of life is sought in the union with the Greater Life, which embraces the transitory world as a matter of course, as well as everything that is contradictory to rational demands for order and value, then tranquillity takes on another meaning. When the limits to man's ability to safeguard his existence and the limits to the supremacy of his mental powers are wisely recognized, he is prevented from falling a victim to their extravagant domination. It is then that the soul's desire for stillness in life as a whole assumes the character of a magnet to which all human endeavour is forced to surrender itself as though drawn by some magic force. This craving can only be satisfied when man acquires a spiritual attitude which no longer allows him to be oppressed by the discrepancies of a purely objective world. Such an outlook requires that the very source of all contradiction must be mastered: The ego and its concern for personal safety and the mind's concern for lasting achievements are consigned to their proper proportions: they are made subject to a deeper Self, in which man, reunited to the Greater Life, lives and dies, pursuing his work with a tranquillity which is as that of Nature herself.

The European, too, knows that the consummation of his life is the repose of his soul in God. Tranquillity as the result of union with God has not, however, been made the motive force of his life on earth. This only happens when he has tired of self-indulgence, of pursuing the impulse to develop his own personality, of trying to safeguard his ego, and achieve mental distinction, and is preparing himself for the 'homeward path'. It is the nature of a European as against an Oriental to be a creature who is constantly departing; the nature of the latter is to be constantly returning homeward. Man stands always at the crossroads of departure and homecoming. His individual character determines whether he is going to seek himself and God on his way out or on his way home. A European is inclined to listen to the call of the world, living his life in it and submitting himself to its laws, and only experience a desire to return when his one-sided point of departure has proved a failure. An Oriental usually becomes aware far sooner of the appeal of his nature to refrain from asserting himself in the world in an active manner, and begging him to look for his true home within himself. If he does that and renews his contact with the Greater Oneness of life, he may be entrusted with the task of bringing salvation instead of reform into the world, and leading it back to its source. The mystery of Great Union does not lie at the close of life in the East, nor does understanding only come through suffering and failure in other spheres: man possesses and cherishes it throughout his life as an inborn blessing and experience. The Oriental has not fallen as far, as it were, from life's original unity as the Westerner; his individuality and rational powers are less conspicuous. In so far as this is the case, he is the 'younger' of the two. If his 'ego-mind' begins to assert itself independently, his primordial contact with life as an undivided unity does not hesitate to inform him that this assertion of his ego or claim to 'valid' patterns of thought are antagonistic to his basic union with life. Opposition sharpens his response to deep-set unity and instead of allowing his ego and his intellect a free hand he submits them both to its service. And so he begins to strive after stillness as a path towards all-embracing unity from an early age, not waiting for old age to crave for it. In so far as the East has submitted to this attitude over a long period of time it must be said that it is 'older', that is, wiser and more mature than the West. A cult of tranquillity can only become a dominating factor when man comes to realize life's purpose when still in his prime, the purpose which is to be found in tranquillity.

Man experiences 'tranquillity' in many different ways. He experiences it as temporary satisfaction, as meeting his need to safeguard his own individuality; as a spiritual being he experiences it when he apprehends some perfect structure. Every human being feels naturally drawn to these forms of tranquillity. Yet they are merely temporary states, moments of happiness in a life which seeks its purpose not in that deep oneness which is beyond all oppositions, but in the juxtaposition of concrete things whose susceptibility to change is a further incentive to him. Beyond all these there is the experience of tranquillity as an expression of that unity of existence which transcends all mutual opposition of subject and object. It can become the point of departure and the ultimate aim of all spiritual development and all behaviour, in so far as it really is experienced and is not just a mere conception or presentiment. It can be made into an 'exercise' whose fruit is not just a passing state but a permanent possession for the 'mature'. 'Maturity' means being in a state of mind where one can perceive harmony in disharmony, and the Great Unity in opposition, whenever 'departure' includes the 'coming home' and man can leave his home without the fear of losing contact with it. The Japanese cult of tranquillity aims at acquiring and maintaining this state of mind and the exercises of this cult are its vital nerve.

2

The nature of Japanese exercise

THE fact that Japanese cultural instincts are more concerned with 'being' than with 'doing', i.e. with the 'way' rather than the 'work', is expressed in his concept of 'exercise'. We are inclined to think of exercise as training in some particular art or ability, that is, the technique necessary for a specific performance, and only to think in second place of *exercitium*. For the Japanese exercise is synonymous with the way to inner maturity, even when he is engaged in acquiring a specific ability. So much is this the case, that on meeting a person he considers to be mature he immediately inquires as to the exercise he has been using. For us, exercise aims at achievement, for the Japanese, at maturity. So we are led to the discovery of an important phenomenon, and it is time for the European to realize anew, or perhaps for the first time, that maturity is potentially inherent in the pursuit of all exercise.

Human life is full of activities which become automatic, and can only be performed in a perfect manner through practice. All of us as children were forced to practise sitting, standing, and walking until we 'knew how', and similarly talking, reading, and writing. Later on in life man attempts various skills, such as the pursuit of sport, a craft or one of the arts ; a high degree of skill in any occupation presupposes training. Yet where do we find training which aims at developing the inner life and not at particular accomplishments, and which does so from the outset and not just late in life?

Perfection presupposes practice. Given the necessary talent, a skill is developed by constant repetition, that is, an ability is created which was not there before. Two factors are contained in every exercise, the one referring to the object and the other to the subject modifying our world and modifying ourselves. Practice aims at an objectively determined achievement and at its prerequisite, the training of some ability. From the point of view of the objective achievement,' ability' is only a necessary prerequisite and technique simply a means to the real end.

The purpose of exercise can, however, be seen as the training of ability or indeed training generally and not as the individual achievement. In sport, for example, any one performance depends on the development of physical and mental propensities which are required for any performance, and the development of all such propensities as are exercised in the pursuit of sport. The pursuit of sport contributes to man's general physical and psychological training. A boy who refuses to see any use for Latin in later life is told that it is an excellent exercise in 'thinking'. But even where the emphasis is placed on the subjective and not in the objective aspect of achievement and training, as here, the reference is always to performance. We are concerned with forming abilities or propensities in order to 'have' more and be able to 'do' more. The fact that a man 'has' more and can 'do' more does not mean that he 'is' more. An exercise, however, does exist which looks beyond the development of mere ability.

In every pursuit, besides the prospect of being able to perform something perfectly and cultivating one's talents in general, apart from any specific achievement, there is yet a third prospect, the chance to broaden one's outlook as a human being and attain to a greater degree of maturity. Each 'exercise' contains the quality of being able to raise the level of a man's mind so that he is able to taste still more elevated experience. It should increase his own effectivity rather than heighten the degree of perfection in his performance of the exercise. This is true experience and is the manner in which he becomes 'effective' out of his essential being: this does not lie in the fact of his possessing certain abilities but in his releasing and cultivating his personal nature.

Any activity in which a man is unpractised makes him aware of tension between the subject, which desires something but is as yet unable to realize it, and the object withholding itself from him. This tension prevents harmonious execution. A man attains technical perfection through long practice so that he can now do something without any conscious effort; whatever the sphere he now feels a sovereignty of mind in having surmounted the original subject-object tension, that is, the discrepancy between initial inability and the object of endeavour. On the basis of this initial tension or discrepancy he feels a sense of 'release' or deep satisfaction at the harmony of subject and object which he has achieved through exercise. This satisfaction is at the same time an indication of a factor of extreme significance.

Ability acquired by practice becomes automatic and its exercise is undisturbed by subject-object tension. Harmony or unison, although implicit, is now no longer experienced consciously. According to the degree in which our consciousness in any activity is influenced by such tension harmony is necessarily excluded. We experience it in the first moment of successful execution of an exercise, the more so since long practice has made us feel tension like a sort of painful spur, forcing us to go on trying to gain release. A means to experience unison is to perform some exercise. When once we have achieved release, we make the all-important discovery that consciousness of unison coincides with disappearance of tension between the subject and the object. Tension, however, may only be eliminated by technical perfection. Absolute unison is impossible as long as the subject is forced to 'will' and man to act as a subject separated from its object, yet at the same time directed towards it. Not until the subject ceases to strive and the object to be attained no longer appears as a separate entity, is this wonderful experience of unison resultant on successful execution possible. Only technical ease which dispenses with the subject can achieve this. Only a man whose mind is set on achieving something can overlook in his haste the ensuing gratification and significance. It is a discovery of very great importance that true unison depends on activity being carried out without the participation of the ego. This is a mark of the inherent depth of every individual existence, in which every natural process is part of the Greater Oneness of life. Initially man acts as an ego, but when he develops beyond the bounds which this imposes on him, he is then enabled to attain to an enjoyment of cosmic harmony and to experience on a higher plane the Great Oneness which hitherto has of necessity been hidden to him. It is thus a long road from the first experience of harmony on the occasion of his first successful performance of his exercise to its physical and psychological prerequisites being permanently fixed in a mental attitude. This is the road of all Japanese exercises which all have the same aim —to make man mature.

Whereas the average individual in the West sees achievement in front of him or the ability which makes this achievement possible, in Japan achievement is only secondary to the ultimate purpose of exercise. On the other hand stress is placed on the opportunity offered by automatic technique of becoming aware of unison outside one's ego. The tendency is prevalent among us to fear for personal values when technique becomes automatic, for now spontaneous tension of the subject and its volition is reduced to a minimum, as for example in the mechanization of modern labour. When this happens, the Japanese recognizes and avails himself of the chance to partake in such harmony utterly devoid of ego, and to safeguard by further exercise that frame of mind which is the prerequisite of personality in his sense. Man must first succeed in finally destroying the spell of the subject-object opposition which shuts him off from the unity of existence. Only in so far as he does this, can permanent enjoyment of that ultimate Oneness take place which permeates him freely and becomes conscious in him whenever he experiences harmony. Man's technical mastery proves his union with the former. He has become, so to speak, a pervious organ of life. Just as the experience and verification of the unity of the Greater Life reveals the significance of the Lesser, so too does the significance of maturity lie in man's being progressively transformed until he attains to a frame of mind which manifests the Great Life. For the Japanese exercise is a way to such transformation—to the attaining of maturity.

If the transformation of the ego into an organ of reality becomes the purpose of life, then the antithesis of pure subjectivity and 'objective' creations ceases to prevail. Every 'object' can be made the theme of an exercise and thereby an occasion of becoming 'a true human being'. A wise old Japanese once remarked to me:

'If something is to acquire religious significance, it need only be simple and capable of repetition.'

27

Simple and capable of repetition! Our daily life is full of such things. Simple tasks done over and over again every day are for us only the prerequisite of real tasks. The Japanese sees them in this light, too, but they mean more to him: they offer him the opportunity to experience what he considers really 'essential'. He makes unconscious automatization both conscious once more and the object of an 'exercise in experiencing unison'; more than that, he makes them into an exercise in developing that general frame of mind which sees such experience as the purpose, and the loyalty to its true meaning as the motive force, of life as a whole. The most natural actions are then made the object of particular exercises—walking, standing, sitting, breathing, eating and drinking, writing and speaking and singing. The arts, furthermore, are the occasion of special exercises, in which the various efforts in a particular 'work of art' are really only different exercises in the one 'way'. This is the way of humanity, or the way of maturity, the way to Tao. The different arts of combat, such as shooting, fencing, and wrestling, are divorced from their concrete object, which is to overcome an opponent, and assume the character of opportunities to acquire the attitude in which the mature man 'conquers without ever fighting'. Where his ego is suspended and he on the one hand achieves his objective effortlessly, and on the other hand just because he does not put his ego forward, he robs his opponent of his 'object'. His opponent shoots, strikes, in the 'void'—and is beaten! A pupil strives in endless repetition to create a perfect work, whether in the arts of painting, flower arrangement, singing, story-telling, forging of swords, or ceramics. At the same time he knows that perfection can only be achieved if he, as the creator, dies to himself and becomes an 'organ of life' rid of his ego. The Great Unity then begins to manifest itself in the language of the image which represents it and to be emanated in the living form which has been created by the hand of man. This in effect is the sole concern of man: to become such an organ. This is the meaning of the Japanese saying that everything is fundamentally alike, archery and dancing, fencing and arranging flowers, painting and wrestling, drinking tea and singing. From the point of view of performance and 'doing', this phrase is meaningless; but as a mark of maturity in which the Greater Life reveals itself more and more perfectly in the Lesser, its meaning is simple and clear.

3

The basic exercises in tranquillity

ALL forms of exercise have the same aim: to establish man in that basic unity which is revealed to him in his experience of unison, when the gap between subject and object is bridged, and he is enabled to preserve harmony in himself. Its loss is synonymous with tension, unrest, and lack of interior peace; its discovery with that deep tranquillity which reveals the essence of life. Every exercise is fundamentally an exercise in tranquillity. Conversely every exercise in tranquillity is fundamentally an exercise in the experience of unison.

The whole life of the Japanese is filled with the exercises in tranquillity. They reach their highest form in the contemplative exercises of the Zen monks; they flourish in all the master schools and form part of the everyday life of the people. The exercise in tranquillity exists therefore at three different levels; on the highest level it is directly concerned with the work of salvation, that is, preparing man to experience the Great Enlightenment (Satori). In the master schools it introduces and forms the basis of the exercises which had a specific object in view. Among the people it forms the basis of their general attitude towards life, and it is perhaps the chief characteristic of Japanese culture that practically every act in daily life is made the subject of an exercise. All of these centre on the pursuit of stillness.

The basic exercise in tranquillity is threefold, the exercise in the immobility of the body, in the breath, and in the centre.

The exercise in the immobility of the body

We have only to hear the phrase to conjure up pictures of Eastern monks and holy men spending hours, days, weeks, or even years, sitting motionless with their legs crossed or in various other postures. Whenever we think about such things we cannot free ourselves of the feeling that to submit to perfect idleness in this manner must surely mean to miss the true purpose of life. We feel that a man who does so has no right to existence. The East sees matters in another way. To sit perfectly still and surrender oneself completely to stillness, whether of the body or the mind, is not synonymous for the Japanese with robbing the gods of time; quite the reverse, he sees it as giving the divine element in us time to become a reality. To let our body, our soul, and our mind become tranquil is not idleness, it is work of the most difficult kind, it means directing oneself through discipline towards real life. Life is 'unreal' as long as man is fundamentally troubled by tension between subject and object in his own outlook. To become tranquil is the way to mature life.

It seems strange to us that absolute immobility of the body should be the means of attaining maturity, because we are hardly able to imagine the soul's being able to be elevated independently of a similar movement of the mind. To assert that a purely physical exercise can have such psychological significance is antagonistic to the idea of the dignity of the mind and soul. In this we are the victims of the domination of our ego through which original unity is split into the opposing poles of body and mind. This division controls our consciousness so absolutely that the original unity of body and soul appears to us either as a lost state of bliss or a mere hypothesis. Today we are once again on the verge of seeking the source of all human life in that original unity. But, blinded as we are, we are afraid to enter the infinite realms which reveal themselves to our inner eye while they remain hidden where the all-dividing light of ego-consciousness prevails.

In the night-light of the depth of the consciousness, which has been preserved to a greater extent in the East, contact with the original unity of *physis* (Nature) and *psychē* (soul) has not been lost, in spite of the tension existing in the day-light of the surface consciousness. Beyond this the people of the East have perceived that in practising absolute immobility of the body they are also practising that tranquillity which is in close proximity to tasting true unity. Thus this exercise is not merely concerned with externals; above all it leads us inward to the One in which our human nature is anchored.

We have to understand this, when we find people everywhere in the East engaging in complete bodily stillness, particularly among the Japanese whose minds and bodies are so very alert. It is awe-inspiring how still these people can stand and sit. They can do it for hours on end. Men and women, old and young, all seem to delight in every opportunity of practising perfect stillness.

What takes place when people sit perfectly still? It is very difficult to put into words. If anyone should make the effort to practise bodily immobility, even if only for half an hour over a few weeks, he will have some strange experiences. They will not only be unusual; their nature is such that, if he is at all receptive to such things, he will be induced to keep on his exercises indefinitely. At first he will be amazed at the extent of his own restlessness, at the variety of conflicting emotions which make themselves felt, and at the stream of unconnected thoughts and images which seize control of his mind. He will be horrified at the amount of distractions and involuntary movements which destroy quietness almost as soon as he has attained it, at the clamour within himself, and the abysses rising up out of his subconscious. If he does persevere—and to do this requires both faith and patience—he will feel his inner rebellion gradually subside, not because he starts to get tired and fall asleep, but because our essential being is gradually brought forth by bodily stillness. It exists prior to and beyond the sphere of all images and thoughts, instincts and impulses, and beyond the antithesis of subject and object, transcending and embracing them all. It is the union with this original essence which is our real concern. In absolute awareness, that is, with his consciousness heightened rather than reduced, man must unite himself with the elemental; according to the degree in which he achieves this, he attains to that inner stage and is liberated from all disturbance whether through limitations, multiplicity, or various antagonisms. Step by step he achieves an outlook on life which imbues such antagonisms and limitations in man's natural existence with a new and wonderful significance. The instincts and the senses, the soul and the mind, the ego and the world are fused and preserved in the basic unity which—in so far as man becomes aware of it—prevents any one of them from becoming dominant, or the obstinacy of any from disturbing the harmony of the whole.

If performed perseveringly and in the right attitude this practice results in a man's enjoying a new and fundamental dimension of life. This takes place during the actual exercise itself, and also, if continued over a number of years, it produces a frame of mind which is no longer in danger of being upset by the turbulence of the ego in its efforts to attain an object. Once in possession of this outlook, man continues to enjoy the stillness of perfect unison in the midst of the changes and unrest which life brings. Tranquillity spreads from its hidden origin up to the surface, reflecting Life undisguised and thus allowing man to recognize a universal law in everything.

The exercise of the breath

Exercise of the breath is quite inseparable from that of immobility of the body. Even with us breathing tends to be discussed more and more frequently, although this is usually with the object of increasing man's efficiency by training his breath. Thus regulating a man's breath and increasing its volume is used as a means of making him more alert, while cramp and tension are relieved by relaxation through breathing exercises. In the East exercises in breathing are not concerned with increasing productive ability nor with relieving tension by learning to relax. Elasticity and relaxation are both but the consequence of a third factor, which is itself the source of still further experiences.

Anyone who has tried to observe his natural breath and consciously perform the act of breathing will be not a little astonished to see how his breath is suddenly and unnaturally disturbed by the very fact of its being put under observation. He has hardly regained his composure when he notices how every single thought, image, or conscious feeling spoils its natural rhythm. The whole aim is to learn to acquire and preserve perfect rhythm of breath, at the same time being fully aware of what is taking place within one. Numerous methods exist, but the one used is less important than perseverance in pursuing the exercise. The essence of all such endeavour is for man to be wholly aware and gradually attain to a state of 'self-lessness' in which he is released from the division of subject and object which ordinarily dominates his consciousness. In that state he can finally experience the perfect enjoyment of the unity inherent in it. He may even taste the joys of an experience which determines all further experience: 'It is not I who am breathing, "it" breathes and I merely have a share as a union of body and soul.' The moment the ego ceases to predominate over the conscious act of breathing, there slip away all opposition and barriers which man's ego has created and fed, and which hitherto have held sway over his physical and mental existence. Now his existence within the narrow limits of the body and his own egocentric mind is gradually transformed or perhaps liberated to the infinity of some greater being. And so he comes to experience tranquillity of the Greater Life. It is as though man had felt himself till now as a wave and, in a tortuous effort to preserve his own self in the continual rise and fall, should suddenly become conscious of the fact that he too is sea and that the sea remains constant whether its waves are in motion or at rest.

Here again the basic Oneness is experienced. At first it is just incidental, but, as the initiate becomes adept, his experience gains stability and becomes rooted in a permanent attitude, so that a man is increasingly enabled to preserve the tranquillity which manifests the 'One', even in everyday life. As to his skill (which we in the West always tend to emphasize), it has not diminished in any way, it has increased in fact, since man has overcome the predominance of his ego and stopped the constant drain of his energy as a result of subject-object tension. The experience of his 'origin' emanating from his essential being increases his confidence in himself. His instinct for self-preservation diminishes, his actions are now more direct and his emotions are no longer inhibited.

Exercise of the breath is practised in Japan by the whole people. The most mature practise it continuously; it is the basic training for all the arts and forms a natural part of the everyday exercises of women and men. A peasant or a worker who has pursued this exercise from childhood will perhaps be disinclined to give information on the subject or to talk about it. But whoever has had the good fortune to have exercised under proper guidance will have no difficulty in recognizing others who do the same.

It must be added that there is an inherent danger in the exercise of the breath or immobility of the body if it is performed without proper guidance. The Westerner may be drawn into experiences for which he is quite unprepared, even though he has humanly speaking the same right to them as an Easterner has. His whole development has been antagonistic to what these exercises aim at achieving; for he has been trained to aim at concepts and things which are clearly distinguished from one another, whereas the East wishes to help men to find the way to the totality which exists prior to all division. Thus he may experience things here which will have a tremendous impact on him. Barriers are lifted and forces released, which raise him for a time on to a plane of ecstatic sensation, only to hurl the uninitiated into an abyss of despair. Bereft from his habitual frame of mind, and as yet not in full possession of the new basis, he is thrown with unwonted abruptness on to reality; he is swamped by the totality which has taken possession of him and which threatens to engulf him, since he has not yet become an organic part of it. This does not mean that exercise of this kind is antagonistic to the nature of the European, but merely shows how far his own development separates him from the experience of ultimate unity. To dwell in the latter or even to give it precedence before the ordered phenomenal world in which it is manifest can perhaps never become the object of Western life. Yet every human existence which continues to live without experiencing the meaning of such unity will be in danger of missing the way of salvation.

The exercise of the centre of being

The exercise of the centre of being! To speak of 'centre' is to conjure up an image of a circle possessing a central point which is in a certain relation to the periphery. The periphery is 'outside', the centre inside, representing depth as opposed to superficiality. All points on the periphery are related to the centre equally; viewed from the centre they are all eccentric. Movement from the centre to the periphery is centrifugal, that from the periphery to the centre is centripetal. The periphery can revolve in circular motion while the centre remains motionless, governing all surrounding movement as a whole. We experience each of these aspects in the exercise of the centre as they affect ourselves. We say of people that they are 'centred' or that they are eccentric, meaning that their way of life is in harmony with their essential being, or conversely that a lack of proportion prevents them from being themselves and endangers their individuality. Everyone possesses his own formula as to the relation between centrifugal and centripetal motion, but it seems to be generally accepted that the rhythm of such motion is to be determined from the centre and not from the periphery.

If we should set about the exercise of the centre in the same form of consciousness as we would any other task, in other words, with the ego asserting itself as the subject and accordingly determining and fixing the thing to be done as object, we will not be spared an unpleasant experience.

37

In our efforts to find the centre within ourselves, the more determinedly our ego asserts itself and causes us to make ourselves into an object and to adhere hard and fast to this object, the result will only be for us to reach a painful state of rigidity in which all life comes to a standstill. We would experience in an almost unprecedented manner in our own person the extent of the threat offered by the forces of the ego, which turn the living natural world into so many dead 'factors'. We are not here concerned with the question as to how far the human mind and its talent for creative activity is rooted in this ability of the ego; we are only concerned with its negative aspect, that when man regards himself from the viewpoint of the ego he becomes the victim of his own reflection. But man is more than just an ego, and therefore, if he takes himself and his ego's instinct to be the central point seriously while practising the exercise of the centre, he will perceive life coming to a standstill in himself. This experience may be accompanied by a serious shock, when all of a sudden he feels unable to escape from the state of rigidity forced on him by his ego. It is not possible here to examine how this painful state may be overcome and gradually outgrown. It depends in all cases on the novice relinquishing his own small self as the subject of his search for a centre. If he succeeds in doing this through conscious meditation (not concentration!) he will feel the rigidity in himself giving place to some new centre. This new centre is quite distinct from that other one, which in reality was nothing but the ego, identical with itself and reflecting its own identity eternally. He now experiences the centre of his being as something far more than his own ego, far more than just 'he himself'. Having succeeded in attaining it he now discovers everything being submitted to it and made a harmonious part of it in such a manner as to transcend the tension between subject and object. Everything is now centralized in perfect harmony with the systole and diastole of the universe.

We all know something of this state of being from those fleeting moments in life when we suddenly feel as if we were 'rounded off' and can perform whatever we have to do with perfect ease. Everything seems in its proper place and we can accept in perfect equanimity disturbances which at another time might have deeply distressed us. It is not until this sensation is destroyed by some sudden thought or emotion that we are thrown once more into the old 'decentric' tension of subject and object, and it is only by sheer 'concentration' of the will that we can master the situation. Life from the living centre is replaced by life governed from the periphery. The exercise of the centre aims at giving us as a lasting possession something that we ordinarily only experience as a passing happy moment—occasionally, for example, on awakening— as the gift of chance, of whose significance we are hardly aware. This is the exercise of becoming a 'hinge' which remains motionless even when the door is turning on it—to use an image from the German mystic, Master Eckhart, which the Japanese to whom I mentioned it felt to be a perfect designation for what they themselves experienced in their exercises of the centre.

The exercise of the centre is integrally linked with those of immobility and of the breath and lies at the core of all Japanese education. The Japanese has a special word for the centre of body and soul: *Hara*. The number of expressions in which it is found indicates its importance for him. There are master schools that make *hara* the sole object of their exercise, while every master art in Japan considers that it is necessary to possess it in order to achieve 'success' in whatever one is doing.[1] To the Japanese, what a man experiences in the 'centre of being' is none other than the unity of life, bearing all, permeating all, nourishing and enfolding all. Our consciousness is ego-centred and thus separated from the true centre: the purpose of these exercises, of immobility, of the breath, and of the centre of body and soul, is to help us to regain it.

So much for the basic exercises in tranquillity. They are, as we have shown, the property of the whole people, which practises them faithfully to a greater or lesser degree of awareness. Should they forget them, they receive a constant stimulus from the example and teachings of their masters in all walks of life. In some way or another the whole people is acquainted with the great hinge on which the gates of life turn, with the sea which casts the waves on the shore, and with the calm mirror of the depths, which reflects everything in its own proper place.

4

How tranquillity stands the test of life

EVERY 'exercise' has a twofold aim: it aims at establishing us in our 'true element' and at eliminating anything that could stand in the way of the latter. Whatever its form or its theme, an exercise is always directed at establishing us securely in the totality of the Greater Life, to which the death of the ego is a necessary precondition. A prisoner in the shell of the ego is a prey to attack from within and without. Once united with his origin he is impregnable. As long as he is subjected to the ego he is a plaything of all destructive forces, but freed from it is a fit and powerful protagonist of life. Having once experienced the centre, a man can reveal the meaning of life, whereas, if he is caught in the periphery, he becomes the victim of false illusion.

What we aim to achieve in the basic exercises in tranquillity holds good, in so far as we do achieve it, in any situation in life; we maintain it by cultivating a lasting attitude in which we conduct ourselves not only as *existing* beings, which we also are, but as *essential* beings which we really are. This could not be solely the result of the basic exercises of which we have been speaking. A Japanese once asked me when I pursued my exercises and when I replied, 'for one hour in the morning and in the evening,' he declared that I had not even begun to understand what exercise meant and that, until it went on continually throughout my whole day, I would have achieved nothing. In other words, every single act must be permeated by the composure which exercise produces. This quality must be at the base of every outward manifestation, its driving force and life breath, infusing it with true meaning from the centre. And so a fundamental attitude is the object of all Japanese education and is cultivated in the external composure evinced in daily life. It is of course the basis of the different arts and is joined with the particular 'technique' in each case, culminating in those exercises which aim at man's preparation for his coming redemption.

Every foreigner remarks on the Japanese control of facial expression and on the economy of their movements. They overcome their natural reserve with difficulty; they do not seem receptive to new impressions, or at least only superficially. It is a basic facet of Japanese education to preserve external composure amid life's inconsistencies and defects, and perfect equanimity in natural calamities and in the vicissitudes of fortune. The Japanese is a human being like we are, and he is affected by anger and pain no less than ourselves. Yet he does not rebel against life's being as it is to the same extent as we do. Man's natural instinct for self-preservation is reduced to a minimum in his case and so he does not abandon himself to pain or to anger when life deprives him of some possession or does not live up to his expectations. He seems unmoved by disorder and decay in the round of his daily life, except in the case of objects or places hallowed by tradition or rules laid down by 'authority'; similarly he faces change and the passing of life with genuine equanimity. Beneath his attitude is a natural and humble submission to death as the 'other side' of life. The purpose of every exercise is to enable us to see death as the other side of life and the actual act of dying as the gateway to the Greater Life. Japanese education through the medium of exercise is simultaneously education for death, teaching a man to let his ego die continually. 'Your education is almost exclusively concerned with this life,' a Japanese once remarked to me, 'whereas we educate for life by educating a man for death.' This education proves itself in everyday life: it is prominent in the technical training for the different arts and it culminates in a calmness at death which has so often astonished European missionaries. Fear of death or of the hereafter scarcely exists among the Japanese, since the 'hereafter' can be but the unity of the Greater Life which they have constantly sensed even in this life.

In Japan calm acceptance of destruction and death is not synonymous with weary resignation, with fatalism, or even heroic strength in renouncing life and possessions—as disease, earthquakes, fires, and floods give the Japanese ample opportunity to prove. This calmness is the expression of his experience, long renewed and cultivated against the growing claims of ego and intellect, a realization of man's true nature, which no antithesis of being or non-being, having or not having, becoming or decaying, can ever touch.

Even if he has never performed an exercise, a man who has grown up in the Japanese tradition has some share in this knowledge. But if he does start and introduces deep-set unity into his inner perception by means of certain exercises, and preserves it there over the decades, his acquaintance with 'control of life and death' grows. The greater his success in doing this, the more composed he himself becomes; with natural ease and discipline he fulfils the role allotted to him by his destiny—whether as a farmer, worker, scholar, official, or soldier—and does this with the whole of himself, that is, without any fragment of his ego remaining and trying to achieve distinction for itself.

A foreigner is forcibly struck by the wave of personal ambition in academic and business life in present-day Japan. Contrary to tradition, and to the original rhythm of Japanese life, it is the product of a movement which only set in after the traditional order had begun to dissolve and contact with the civilization of the West had been made. It is indeed a tragic development and one which has involved the Japanese people in a sort of delayed crisis, such as the European has been experiencing for a long time past and which he hopes to surmount with the aid of the ancient forces of the East.

One of the most supreme expressions of the true Japanese outlook was shown in the last war by the Kamikaze pilots. To speak of their performance in such terms as 'patriotism', 'idealism', 'youthful dedication', or 'heroism' is to misjudge them entirely. These pilots, in risking death, proved that a form of human death does exist in the midst of life, and that it exists not only for life's sake, but also for death's sake. There is a manner of dying which transcends the antithesis 'life and death' and which might be termed 'already existing in another life'. Such a frame of mind—and of body also—enables a man to face the most arduous task of his life and even death itself without flinching. He has attained perfect tranquillity without inner resistance, having sacrificed his ego-self—and he now surrenders himself simply to the demands of the moment. He is prepared to give the utmost life demands from him in the situation in which he has been placed, whether a scion of nature, a rational being, or a mature personality. Freed from the shackles of ego, he fulfils the law of being within the limits of his human power and his existence in space and time, which this law transcends. He lives his life as a human being, neither overstepping the bounds of moderation nor underestimating the abilities he does possess. He fulfils the demands of the moment without personal ambition, submitting himself to the order which Nature, history, and fate have imposed on him. His private individuality and the efforts of his mind to achieve objective perfection are held in proper proportion, which includes acceptance of death. When death finally approaches him as life's fulfilment in the particular situation he finds himself, he does not resist. All the master arts teach that death of the ego is the prerequisite of genuine achievement. The Zen monk who has reached the final stage can determine the moment of his own death. He knows when his hour has come and when it is time to pass on into the kingdom where the ego is silent for ever and the soul prepares to continue its journey in another form. Having invited his friends, he seats himself in his accustomed place to write his last poem and then simply does not return from his contemplation, which he performs just as he has done every day of his life.

All genuine Japanese life contains an element of this. It cannot be called 'worldly', cannot be attributed either to this life or to the hereafter, nor be termed 'idealistic' or 'materialistic'. Anyhow, death for the Japanese is not the threatening force it is for us and, similarly, their attitude to life preserves the tranquillity of Nature herself. An animal dies in the forest without a murmur, noiselessly trees and flowers grow to maturity and then cease to exist. In the same way life in Japan is permeated with a natural stillness, of which growth and decay form a necessary part. And so Japanese tranquillity seems to contain something of Nature's own wisdom which acts freely in the mature man, fulfilling in his person the demands which the universal law prescribes for all its creatures. The inner composure here evidenced is cultivated in the exercise of immobility of the body. In practising absolute stillness in this way a man learns to overcome the perils and discrepancies of life without having to assert himself actively against them. More than that, he learns to enjoy the reality which exists beyond life and death, which is a part of Truth itself.

The effects of these exercises are closely allied in daily life with those of exercises in the breath and in the centre of the body and soul. It is a maxim of Japanese philosophy and education never to get out of breath and the Japanese train themselves in such a way, that, should there be any danger of it happening, they can counteract it by having recourse to controlled, rhythmic breathing. Once it has been pointed out to him, a man will never fail to notice how, when the Japanese become excited, they immediately think of their breath and recover their equanimity by exhaling deeply. They do this too before every task in order to become recollected. A man is absolute master of his body and his mind when he has a conscious share in the supreme 'It breathes'. In addition he is aided by something that is not concentration through his own willpower, for the latter is open to attack by unknown forces. He no longer depends absolutely on his own ego, whose tendency to fix everything definitively interferes with the flexibility of perfect activity. The painter and the dancer, the actor and the forger of swords, the potter and the story-teller, the master in the art of tea and the master of the bow, even the business man and the statesman, they all prepare themselves for creative work and decisions by sitting motionless and practising breathing. Sometimes, prior to some important decision, they spend the night in a monastery, in order to converse with the master and give themselves up to contemplation. They do not go there in order to 'meditate' on their own problems, but to surrender themselves to the source of life, whose fluidity relieves a problem of its complexity and allows a man to exercise his own powers in perfect liberty.

It would be foolish to ask how then, despite such an outlook and such knowledge of the hidden laws of life, Japanese statesmanship can make mistakes and why the average Japanese is a human being with all human failings. The Japanese are men as we are, no wiser and no better than ourselves; they are 'on the way' and not yet at their goal. We go astray on our path towards achievement and our ideal of a permanent order and become fanatical and evil, if we sacrifice the religious element to the demands of the moment. In exactly the same way, the East loses sight of external values, if it neglects the objective world and becomes over-preoccupied with the inner meaning of life. We are easily upset by outward failure and we plunge into mental anguish if we forget that our first aim is to become mature. Similarly, a person following the inner way exclusively may well fail when confronted with elemental decisions outside the framework of everyday life.

Our intellect is powerful and constantly exercised and we are therefore accustomed to rapid decisions. In the East up to a short time ago tradition and a slow rhythm of life prevailed in all spheres, and the conservative mind finds it difficult to adapt itself to new demands. We have forgotten the inner life, the East has forgotten external reality as well as the fact that the world is developing and contracting. The results of our mistaken policy confront us once more with the question as to what is the essence of the human soul. The Japanese in their turn are confronted by their failure in the world of today with the age-old problem of how to serve their soul as it would be served, and yet to control the external world through the powers of the intellect. A new life is beginning for the East, as well as for ourselves. There as well as here exclusiveness has precipitated a state of crisis. The long tradition of the creative mind will not, however, be obliterated for our own selves by the necessity of including the inner way; the East must learn to prove its traditional inner serenity within the demands of modern times which are opening up, for the first time in its history, to the mode (*ratio*) of the West. The inherent wisdom of tranquillity is still valid, nor has the importance of exercise which leads up to it been diminished; the traditional view remains unchallenged, that only what evolves from true stillness, which itself emerges from correct breathing, is commensurate with true life.

Many phenomena of Japanese life become intelligible, if they are seen as the effects of these practices, which raise the centre of body and soul, the true centre of gravity, into consciousness and keep it there. The impression is not infrequent that the Japanese moves within the bounds of an inner orbit and, revolving around some mysterious centre, refuses to exceed a set number of human contacts, interests, and emotions. His smiling politeness towards strangers is for the most part only his way of keeping them 'outside', stopping them from coming too near, not to speak of letting them enter. The Japanese guards his inner 'orbit', which he infuses with his personality till it is just full and can hold no more. He does not permit his attention to be taken up with novelties; if something attracts him momentarily, he refuses to allow it to go too deep and is on his guard against inner impulses which might endanger his balance. Men are distinguished from animals by their tendency towards immoderation, which make them consider places and possessions merely as the basis of something further. Among the Japanese, however, even this tendency is either undeveloped or checked in its early stages, and he is therefore less tempted by the human potentialities for control of Nature through technical means. The Japanese is more conscious of the threat of eccentricity and takes it more seriously than we do. If life should draw him away from himself, he rapidly regains control. A man who achieves distinction through his rank, position, ability, or a particular talent, is careful to show in his outward demeanour that his inner life still governs him. But it is above all the Japanese woman whose bearing shows how aware she is of the unifying powers of the centre. She, not the man, is the secret centre of the home. She lives a life more in keeping with the centre than her husband, who is forced into the world by his profession and is distracted by worldly struggles and ambitions. Once his confidence has been won, a Japanese may well tell of how his wife will quietly intercede in a moment of stress, and in her unfathomable silence will smooth out life's tangles and bring order to confusion through the power of the living centre, and how she achieves all this without actually 'doing' anything, without so many words.

5

Objective tranquillity

THE exercises in tranquillity—bodily immobility, breath, and centre—are specifically exercises in an inner state of being. Their powers of development are unlimited. They alone can endow life as a whole in all its various spheres, and at all levels, with a new purpose and a new form. They supply the basic training for an immediate objective, whether creative work or performance. No matter how adept a pupil becomes, he still continues to practise them. Besides these exercises in inner life, which aim at acquiring a specified frame of mind and demeanour, there exist others. Here the principles of life—and it is the supreme object of *all* exercise to establish contact with these—do not appear in the exercises to which we have just referred in the form of a sudden light within ourselves. Instead, they touch us, as it were, from without. We see the source of all modes of being, itself absolute and therefore 'modeless', in a mode which is determined objectively. And that realm, which both transcends and is at the same time the source of all forms, communicates itself to us in the shape of one particular form, and we learn to perceive both the essence and the origin of the plenitude of the phenomenal world in the Great Void, and in the manifold language of life to become aware of the silence of nothingness, in which the words themselves are first formed.

This may become clearer if we think of an experience common to us all: if we are walking alone on a dark night and are suddenly frightened by the call of a bird we become aware of the surrounding stillness in a way we were not before. It begins to speak, is no longer just nothing, but a language intensely alive. The same occurs when a twig breaks under the tread of a deer and all of a sudden the stillness around us is filled by this one sound with the thousand voices of forest life. Perhaps we are enjoying the quiet of a country noon on a calm sunny day and the tolling of a bell reaches us out of the distance; its unexpectedness arouses our consciousness of life pulsating beneath apparent serenity.

These are only fleeting impressions, but they serve to give us momentary experience of what the Japanese cult of tranquillity aims to implant more deeply in us, wherever the latter is exercised in connection with some specific object. We are concerned with seeing or rather perceiving life in its tangible forms, in such a manner as to allow the 'undivided' origin in which all forms are grounded to appear before the eyes of our mind.

The cult of tranquillity has the power to reveal the original language of the phenomenal world to us. Essentially it consists in learning to react to objects, images, and situations in such a way that the mind does not surrender itself exclusively to them, but uses them to attain to the living origin of which they are but the expression. The simplest and best-known example of this is the humming tea-kettle. Both in everyday life and in the tea ceremony itself, an exercise is successful if it helps us to perceive the humming in the right way. For if it is heard in the proper manner, it evokes a characteristic stillness. The pleasant ticking of an old grandfather clock awakens the same response in us. There is a special quality in this. This is the quality which the Japanese aim to acquire. Something special is speaking.

Sometimes one hears that the humming of the tea-kettle reminds the Japanese of rustling pines in a lonely mountain. It is not the rustling itself which is significant, but the serenity which it evokes. Another example frequently referred to with the same affection is that of the sound of a spring in a garden, or water falling constantly from a bamboo cane. It is this sound which brings the house and the fenced garden to life, which together represent a whole pattern of life. Similarly the tranquillity of Nature is perceived in the noise of a waterfall—the deep tranquillity of life in the echoes of a song.

Here we are concerned with one of the many paradoxes of Japanese life, whenever it is necessary to lift the veil which has been placed over the processes of life by the rigidity of the ego. According to the Japanese outlook, the creative mind acts in a manner commensurate with life, when the realm which embraces and transcends all forms— and which thanks to its undivided unity is the true realm of tranquillity—is made perceptible through the medium of its creatures, individual forms; its undivided unity makes it the true realm of tranquillity. To content oneself with the fond illusion that hides true life is to prove oneself still immature.

At this point the difference at a spiritual level from the European becomes very apparent. Tranquillity reaches a European through his mind, as in his quiet enjoyment at the sight of some structure which he has helped to create, filling him with a sense beyond space and time, as always when confronted by perfect or 'classical' form. A perfect work of art rests in itself—'*Das Schöne scheinet in ihm selbst*',* as the poet Mörike says. The beauty of the mind's

*Approximately: 'Beauty is self-sufficient'. The double meaning of *scheinen*—to shine or to appear or seem and the use of the ordinary personal pronoun *ihm* instead of the reflexive *sich* by the poet makes both interpretation and translation problematical.—Translator's note.

creations, the harmonious proportions of a perfect whole, seem to be but a wonderful reflection of the Divine itself. A sense of timelessness elevates us above our ordinary life through our visual or auricular share in such perfection. Our restless efforts are stilled by it, we feel blessed by fulfilment and become absolutely tranquil.

The Japanese spirit and the tranquillity which its 'successful' manifestations evoke do not raise us, as it were, above existence: they rather draw us into its depths. The Japanese is not concerned with 'valid forms' nor compact and perfect structures, although his art does evince these qualities. He is concerned with something that is neither form nor image nor mode, something that shimmers through such forms as are perfect in his sense, communicating itself as the source of life common to both them and us. He values a form all the more for its not trying to hold a man fast in its grip, but brings about a transformation of his mind, and rids him of all forms, so that he senses the Great Harmony. For a form is only valuable so far as its particular language opens the gate to the 'Supreme One' and through its magic force unites man with his origin. The work of a master aims at perceiving this 'Supreme One'. It transcends the individual manifestations or forms of itself, which it evokes and to which they all return, and which is at once the whole of all existing forms.

Certainly another Japanese art does exist in which the motion of life is reflected in a perfect form and the work of art has, as its primary aim, the achieving of objective form in our sense. Of the two poles of life—development towards a perfect individual manifestation and return to original unity—the East gives preference to the latter both by natural inclination and conscious endeavour, and this also determines artistic taste. We see this in the customary form of small objects, in the architecture of the temples and in

53

household goods, the unadorned walls, and the clothes of the educated classes, whose tranquillity to the Japanese is the mark of their 'culture' and who spread stillness in their demeanour. Bright colours belong to the world of children or the uneducated masses; they have a symbolic meaning, as in the theatre, or they betray the parvenu.

Man is to be made aware of life by means of a paradox. This method is used in all the arts, attaining its highest form in the nonsensical *koans* which the master of Zen sets his pupils. The failure of the pupil's rational powers will awaken in him a consciousness of a deeper life. To take the example of the dance: a dance appears artistically perfect to our eyes when the performer conjures up for us the image of a whole through a multiplicity of separate movements. The image is beautiful in itself when the sum of its movements leaves the impression of a harmonious whole. The enchantment of the Japanese dance, on the other hand, lies in the dancer revolving round an invisible axis: it cannot be 'danced' through the art of movement, but it can be made to be felt as the centre which infuses life and purpose. In perfect movement the Unmoved itself can be experienced—the source of each single gesture, uniting and enfolding every one of them in itself. The art of a great master in dancing lies as much in his ability to portray the Unmoved as in the power of his movements around the invisible centre.

Similarly, the strange fascination of Japanese singing lies in its ability to produce an inaudible note, which is at the heart of all notes which are actually sung. The song seems to appear out of eternity and disappear again into it, without beginning or end, awakening in the listener that unsingable note which represents the soundless plenitude— the source of all notes. This primeval note of life is for the listener, as it were, the mother of longing transmitted through the atmosphere of a song. For that longing brings all forms to fleeting perfection only to resume them back into herself. We meet the same thing in a branch of painting —the black-and-white painting which is a product of Zen. With a few strokes a bird is painted on a bare branch and the branch hangs out into empty space; a little boat floats lonely on a great sea, a couple of roofs appear out of the morning mist, or the silhouette of mountains sinking into the dusk, as though they were but the fleeting reflection of some spirit assuming their form for a brief moment. Such pictures are tangible examples of an art whose purpose is to express life's creative yet soothing stillness, through a particular medium. This is not life in its ordinary sense but the one prior to all individual lives existing in and above them all, producing them all as the sea produces its waves and, like the sea, resuming them again. The sea is only visible in its waves. We only become aware of its unfathomable depth when the wave does not make itself absolute but looks on itself as part of its origin, not self-sufficient. Man must do likewise!

The purpose of all form is to reveal what cannot be formed, and which only manifests itself in the reflection of some mind, appearing only to disappear again. In itself, form is nothing. To the receptive, however, it can reveal the intangible source of all being, and lead the mind to the true Law of the Universe. Where that is the case the individual self becomes a direct reflection of the Absolute. A work of art, then, has the power to bring us face to face with the ground of life and produce in us that tranquillity which is the element of living being. As in the case of the various arts, so too the cult of the home in Japan aims at evoking tranquillity. If we remember this we will understand the absolute simplicity of the tea-room for the Japanese. This room, more than any other, breathes stillness. By entering it in the right disposition, a man frees himself from all constricting form. Only the detached mind can experience the purity of true peace which attains its happiest expression in the performance of the ceremony. We do not realize the extent to which Japanese culture has been formed by the atmosphere and ritual of the tea-room. Both in the ritual and in the room itself everything is arranged in such a way as to make us aware of the hidden plenitude of the void. The Japanese has a horror of any rich or bright ornament in his home. The walls are without pictures, the table bare of cloths or the reed floor of a carpet. In the *Tokonoma*, or niche, there is a single roll, which is changed to suit the atmosphere or occasion; beneath it is a flower arrangement or a single *objet d'art*—that is all. The walls are the more eloquent for their bareness. I recall a conversation with an old Japanese who encouraged me to speak of Zen—undoubtedly he wished to test how far I understood it. I had scarcely begun when he shook his head a little and with a significant smile motioned towards the bare walls with a slight gesture: 'Do not say anything!—these say all that is to be said.'

Thus the cult of tranquillity in the realm of created form means letting the Great Silent One speak and the Lightless One shine, in learning to hear the Great Noiseless One and seeing the Invisible One. In everything the Great Void must be made perceptible and the Intangible grasped. It is like the eleventh saying of Laotse's: 'Thirty spokes meet the axle, but it is the space between them which is the true nature of the wheel. Vessels are made from clay but it is the space within which is their true nature. Walls with doors and windows form the house, but the house is actually the space they enclose. Usefulness is based on material things, but the essential on what is "beyond".'

6

Tranquillity in absorption

THE cult of tranquillity fosters the inner life and gives a true perception of the phenomenal world. This is brought about when the antithesis of subjective feeling and objective thought has been overcome. The division into subject and object, rooted in the spirit of the ego, disappears when we begin to listen to our own inner world and to regard the external world in the right way. Additional exercises do however exist, which are expressly concerned to resolve the division of subject and object; on doing so they make use of the experience and effects of their re-union of the antithesis in order to help man come to himself, that is, to become mature. These exercises are taught by the masters and are based on the tasks of everyday life.

A man brought up by the sea or in the mountains is familiar with unforgettable scenes of old fishermen and peasants on holiday. He sees them in his mind's eye, staring motionless for hours on end into Nature, as though absorbed by the rhythms of the waves or the undulating land, and seeming to be a necessary part of life pulsating everywhere. It is of such that we must think, when we see Japanese sitting, hour after hour, contemplating Nature till they seem to lose themselves in her. We must never forget that Zen monks practise contemplation, even at the highest level, with their eyes open. What value would stillness hold, if it meant that we may no longer look on the world? Only an alert eye can perceive lasting things. Only an exercise which succeeds in overcoming the antithesis between the ego and the world, simply because it has itself experienced the whole extent of the opposition, can lead to the unison which can stand the test of an active life.

The exercise of the Great Unison of ego and the phenomenal world finds its most popular and primitive expression in the Japanese bath. The bath is not intended for purposes of washing; this precedes it. It is there for us to become dissolved in, as it were, and totally identified with the element, which hitherto has merely surrounded us in the form of water. This means letting ourselves become consciously one with the object of our exercise. This is the aim of all true contemplation of Nature, like listening to a song in the proper manner, looking at a work of art, enjoying a garden or the sight of a dwarf tree, a flower, or even a stone, as in the correct contemplation of a mandala or a sacred picture.

Everywhere the same thing is practised: an object properly understood reveals in its own particular fashion the Great Oneness. And what of the subject which is in contact with the object? It is no different: in so far as it possesses a true understanding of itself it is nothing but an individual expression of the 'unity in essence'. When a subject and an object come into contact with one another they are as yet separate entities. The 'ego' insists on its existence and so establishes itself and the object as things apart, in such a manner as to make the latter assert *its* entity, as the reflection and opponent of the ego standing in itself. The unity of their common origin can therefore never be evoked. We are to learn the reunion, the emergence of the '*Not-Two*'. This means causing the ego to disappear as an independent unit which transforms the object into an opponent and keeps it as such. We must do this by keeping absolutely still, and while we consolidate ourselves in the centre, surrender to the Great Breath of 'It'. This causes the common origin of the subject and its opponent to be evoked, and each ceases to exist as a self-sufficient unit. Basic unity becomes manifest, 'breaking through', as it were, and all-embracing. A totally new basis has been won, the antithesis of ego and non-ego has disappeared. The minor consciousness of the ego struggling to assert itself now gives place to a deeper consciousness and man is no longer determined by the tension of two stubbornly divided poles. A living polarity vibrates, revealing to the transformed self this unity, in the form of intuition where it observes, of truth where it discriminates, as perfection in its creative work, and unfailingly hitting the mark wherever it performs some act. For 'Truth can only be grasped where knowledge has first passed through the experience of the "One"'. A Japanese thinker once put the following question to me: 'Do you seriously believe that anyone can call himself a "philosopher", or even presume to control men or life without having had at least once such an overpowering experience of ultimate "oneness" that this has become the criterion of his whole thought?'

Who has not known the fleeting joy of such an experience? But few have allowed themselves to be determined by it. Few have learnt to dwell on it, to infuse their distracted existence with its beneficial power. This lies at the root of the radiant, tranquil expression on the faces of Eastern people, which we also sometimes see on the countenance of some old master in his craft. An atmosphere laden with 'being' seems to fill the rooms where archers, fencers, and wrestlers exercise in the presence of the masters. This is to be understood as the mind's being infused with the basic unity, which is also the source of the unique atmosphere of a Japanese theatre, where actors and audience gradually become one.

If we know how to take part in the *Noh* dance and in the *Kabuki* or classical drama we too can witness the spell-like effects on the mass of onlookers, when each movement and each scene becomes gradually imbued with the force of such unity, and, according to the talent of the exponent, communicates itself to the audience quite independently of the play itself. Only in this way can we possibly understand how the whole of life seems to be concentrated again and again in one single gesture, making itself felt as some primeval power, unable to be acted, yet inherent in every act. The tension mounts, hypnotizing the listeners, until, after one breathless moment of utter stillness, the culmination of a series of movements, it seeks outlet in a piercing shriek, which only serves to heighten the impact of the silence that preceded it.

Far more than by receptive observing or listening, the deep unison of stillness as the ultimate expression of life can be experienced in exercises in which a specific *act* is performed. In Europe the best known of these is the tea ceremony, at least from hearsay, although it has as little to do with aesthetic values as a picture of Seshu has with 'beauty' in our sense. Another such exercise is the art of archery.[2] Further examples are fencing, wrestling, painting, dancing and story-telling, arranging flowers, and writing. In every case technique is practised for years on end till it finally comes to mean far more than 'technique' as we know it. One day the tension will be surmounted between an object resisting the subject and the subject as yet incapable of overcoming it. It is only now that the harmony of the whole, the absolute unison of task and technique, results in the perfect act as the fruit of inner maturity—which from the beginning has been the aim of the exercise!

The product of any art which has achieved a degree of mastery is born of the Great Stillness. The intellect is no longer necessary, the will is silent, and the heart is still: ego is dead. The task is performed by 'It', not through the efforts of the ego. 'Supreme being' is manifested in the form of a perfect structure of faultless performance; this has been made possible by man having burned out his subjective feelings, his will, and his intellect in constant exercise, so that he now becomes an ideal medium for the specific manner in which Divine Unity has chosen to reveal itself.

7

The ultimate test of tranquillity

THERE are therefore three forms of exercise: those which are directly concerned with achieving a certain attitude (immobility, breath, and centre), those which aim at the transparence of the phenomenal world, and finally exercises in realization of the '*Not-Two*' through technical ease in creative work or practical achievement. Basically, all these have the same aim, which is a permanent state of mind in which the ultimate unity is revealed and is preserved beyond the present moment. Man becomes himself a medium, through which a ceaseless flow of living being seems to pass, manifesting the universal law in each conscious act. Thus the purpose of all exercise is the mature individual—in the very deepest sense of the word.

Everywhere in the world, when a stranger enters his house for the first time, the peasant submits him to the 'test of tranquillity'. He does not judge him on his introductory words. Noisy gestures or a forceful approach make him suspicious. With his head slightly turned to one side, he listens to the silence emanating from the stranger's individual aura, which has an eloquence of its own, a series of noiseless vibrations which every human being evokes, quite apart from his actions or his words.

The 'test of tranquillity' characterizes all human contact in Japan. A Japanese appears to listen to the words of a stranger with intense interest. With smiles and gestures of agreement he encourages him to continue, and seems to invite him with apparent accord on to the slippery path of self-satisfaction. In actual fact he is really only listening to see if the stranger possesses the quality of stillness. For, if the latter's words, gestures, and expressions are not founded on this quality, he retreats into himself, whereas if his silence is eloquent, and at heart warm and alive, the Japanese drops his own reserve. Foreigners can live for years among the Japanese without noticing this rule. They live in the vain illusion that they have good friends, and when they finally realize that a barrier still exists, they accuse the Japanese of being two-faced. In reality they never knew him.

The art of the masters consists in estimating another, not on his ability or his words, but on the degree and quality of his tranquillity, his composure, and degree of inner maturity.

A mature man breathes tranquillity: he emanates it because he has successfully evoked unity in himself and he can manifest the common origin of all being, since it has become a reality in him in the form of a power to create and to liberate. Without actually 'doing' anything, his presence alone clarifies, orders, heals. His very existence creates and releases. The culmination of this process is therefore not so much a formed personality and self-sufficient entity, which embraces a whole cosmos of established values and reveals itself as such to the world without, as one who is a perfect *medium*. As such he reveals the law of universal unity and the purpose of life in a changing world, unconsciously creating or restoring it as the occasion demands.

Strange and well-nigh unfathomable is the effect of mature Eastern men and women on ourselves: strange and unfathomable for one whose ideal is the perfectly formed personality. The place these people occupy in space is in effect quite empty. There is nothing to 'go on', nothing tangible. No one knows what is taking place within them nor what they will do next. They seem to be fully present and then to disappear into nothing. A word or gesture falls with the unexpectedness of lightning out of a clear sky, and throws a new light on things. And then a smile covers it over, and it is as though nothing had taken place. Beneath it all they remain in powerful silence. One does not find physical rest in their company, but experiences rather a tranquil motion of the soul, which releases and fosters one's own spiritual growth. They remind one of those pictures of ancients of a thousand years of age with the mountain wind blowing through them, or perhaps of the pictures of Buddha, who seems to have concentrated life in its entirety in his own person in the form of wisdom and love and given it expression in tranquillity.

'Maturity? What maturity is . . .' replied Satomi Taka-hashi, the philosopher of Sendai, in answer to my question on one occasion; he was silent for a moment and said then with a quiet smile: 'The whole expanse of tranquillity.'

8

Conclusion

Have we only been speaking of the East, of Japan? This is true, as far as the images are concerned and the form in which man seeks his own path. But are not these forms and the desires they express our own, too? Are they not characterstic of the human race as a whole? This is what we believe, and we have therefore omitted any learned references to the relation of our thesis to Japanese religion, history, landscape, or race. Is it not true to say that different images in the East appeal to us so much because our own existence as individuals has become so disproportionate to life as a whole? We have our way of life, and the East has its way, which we cannot simply adopt or even imitate without further consideration. Perhaps, however, we may look into the mirror of the East and its manner of seeking and living life in its entirety, and, in doing so, come to realize why our way of being misses the whole of life. It is like the birch tree looking at the beech and thinking only with pride of its own white bark. Gradually, however, it begins not only to sense its own whiteness, but also to feel that it is something more than just a birch tree; it is a *tree*, too; if it continues to think of its bark alone, it may easily forget that the whiteness is destroyed and the foliage withers, if the roots are neglected.

Finally: a basic outlook on life has been cultivated in

the East—in different forms and for different ends—for thousands of years past, and on the pre-eminence of this outlook her whole civilization has depended. Yet this very identical outlook is also to be found in the West, as the guiding principle of particular individuals at particular times, and as the counterpoint of our development as a whole. We have only to realize this more fully, reviving ancient traditions and seeking new ways of restoring it, while we keep in mind the sayings of our own great men.

It was Goethe who said: 'If you become still, help is already at hand,' and Master Eckhart who taught that God speaks His eternal word only to the truly tranquil soul. Of that great seeker of truth, Søren Kierkegaard, it was said:

'As his prayer became more and more recollected, he himself had less and less to say. Finally he became quite still. In his tranquillity, he became more than just a non-talker, he became a listener. At first he had believed that to pray meant to talk, but he learnt that prayer was not even silence: it was listening. And so it is: prayer is not hearing oneself talk. Prayer is becoming still, remaining still and waiting till one hears God.'

ADDENDA

THREE JAPANESE TEXTS

'The Right to Fight'

A Japanese story, related by Tera Sasamote

Two young spear-fighters were standing together in the interval between exercises. They were the disciples of an old master, Gen-no-ju Yamawaki, and they were discussing the best pupil among them, the youth Iori Yagasawa.

'The master has refused again!'

'How strange. And he thinks so much of him.'

'If it had been one of us. But to refuse Iori!'

'When Yagasawa is looked on as the best spear-fighter in Yedo.'

'They say he can beat every master from the other schools!'

'Iori Yagasawa is considered the best contestant since our school began, not just among the contestants of today.'

'That means more than a thousand pupils.'

'I do not know. They say there was once one as good as he, about ten years or so ago. They talked at that time of the master's wanting to make him his successor eventually.'

'And what happened to him?'

'One day he went away and did not return. There is some rumour that he became a priest.'

At these words Iori Yagasawa entered the room. He was heated from exercise and perspiration covered his forehead. He was a handsome youth, with thick eyebrows and clear, shining eyes. He had strong lips and powerful features.

Respectfully he approached the master who was sitting quietly on his cushion, as was his wont, with his elbow resting lightly on the arm support. It had become quite still. Yagasawa knelt down to greet the old man, who, despite his seventy years, was a picture of health.

Iori's two hands were resting on the mat as he knelt before the master. 'Master . . .'

The 'old man with the silver beard' turned calmly towards his disciple. A gentle smile stole into his eyes as he asked: 'Well? The duel again, Iori?'

'Yes, Master. Forgive me for coming with it to you again. But I want to ask you just once more, just once: Agree to contest with me!'

'But, Iori, have I not told you so often? Do not press me!'

This was the fifth time since the beginning of the summer exercises that Iori had begged the master to contest. Each time Gen-no-ju had refused. He had always given Iori his will in everything else. But he had persisted in his refusal of the duel.

'Iori, a Samurai who knows his art must have perfect mastery of himself as well as his art.'

'Yes, Master. I am perfectly aware of this teaching.'

'Perhaps, Iori, but that is not as easy when one is young.'

'Forgive me, Master, if I contradict, but I always have your teaching in my heart. I act day and night in accordance with it.'

It was indeed true that Iori's conduct was such that no one could have said anything bad of him. No one could have accused him of any breach of the rules of the school.

'No, Iori, I do not overlook the seriousness of your efforts; it is indeed unusual how you . . .'

'. . .'

'But we are concerned with much more than just "conduct". You see, you can reach the stage where you are able to get the better of every robber who attacks you in the mountains. But the really difficult thing is to get the better of the devil in oneself.'

'. . .'

'Do not be so impatient, Iori. We will leave it at that—a little while yet, not yet, Iori.'

In his own mind Iori was certain that, one day, he would receive the honour of duelling with the master if he continued in his endeavours to follow his teaching. Gen-no-ju was already old. Iori

70

hoped and prayed that his dream would be fulfilled while the master was still strong. And so he tried again.

'Master, perhaps I am going too far, but I beg you not to refuse, if I ask you once more, if I ask you for the very last time to——'

Iori seemed determined not to give in.

'Well then . . .'

Gen-no-ju observed his determination and his despair; he had closed his eyes as was his habit in moments of great seriousness. Iori did not dare to breathe. . . .

The servant girl entered without a sound and lit the lights.

Somewhere the autumn flies began to sing. . . .

Gen-no-ju seemed to be in the throes of a difficult decision.

Then he opened his eyes calmly and said:

'If you are absolutely determined, I shall grant your request. . . .'

'Master, thank you.' Iori's handsome face became suddenly hot and animated. Almost solemnly Gen-no-ju continued:

'But first . . .'

'Yes?' Iori's heart missed a beat.

'You must contend with someone else.'

Iori flushed crimson.

'With someone else? With whom?'

'With Tesshin, the hermit monk who lives in the precincts of the Genkuji temple in Tahara-machi Asakusa.'

Iori had been Gen-no-ju's disciple for six or seven years now, but this was the first time he had heard the name of Tesshin from the lips of his master or any of the other pupils.

'Tesshin from the Genkuji temple?'

'Yes, when you have vanquished him, I am ready to contend with you.'

'Thank you, Master, thank you.' In his excitement he added a little confusedly:

'What sort of a man is this Tesshin?'

'How can I tell you that now? Just one thing, Iori. Be prepared. He is no easy opponent . . . this Tesshin.'

Full of impatience, Iori awaited the monk Tesshin in his father's house. Each short moment seemed to him a long hour. At last he came. Iori entered the reception room with a beating heart. A rather short man of about forty years was kneeling in a shabby garment near the entrance of the room of the Forty Mats: Tesshin, the priest.

Iori knelt down, bowed, and greeted him:

'I am Iori, second son of Yagasawa Yamatonokami. I am overcome by your kindness in coming such a distance to me, when it was surely my place to go to you. . . .'

Tesshin answered the respectful greeting with a light nod. 'I am Tesshin. Thank you for your invitation.'

'No, it is I who have to thank you, Master.'

'It is a long time since I left my hermitage—and it is quite a distance from Asakusa to Honjo, isn't it?'

In spite of the polite smile accompanying his words, there was not the slightest attempt to offer an excuse for having kept his host waiting over an hour. There was an element of mockery in his whole bearing. Iori felt the same confusion and annoyance as he had on the day when he sent a messenger to Tesshin and had asked him about the priest.

A day after the master's agreeing to contend with him, on the condition that he had first vanquished Tesshin, Iori had sent a messenger to the priest. He told him the circumstances and asked him to contend with him. As the priest's own room was so small and, besides, so many pilgrims visited the temple at Genkuji, he had invited him to come to him. But Tesshin had refused outright. He declared that he was a priest and had nothing to do with the arts of war. But Iori was not the type to give up easily. On the fourth request, Tesshin replied that he would at least come and see Iori.

'As I informed you through my messenger, I am only following the directions given me by my Master; I wish to challenge you to a duel with spears. I beg you to fulfil my request.'

Tesshin replied to this: 'I too have informed you through the messenger that I am a priest and therefore no fit opponent for you in a duel. I pray you to forgive me.'

'I respect your words, but it is my Master's direction. Do not refuse me and——'

'No, the days when I held a spear in my hands are but a dream of the past. Now they hold the holy rosary and are folded in prayer. It is quite out of the question for me to cross spears with a hot-blooded youth like yourself.'

Iori's blood began to boil.

'But I wish that you make an exception in my case and grant me——'

'I seem to perceive some artifice of the Master Yamawaki behind it all. I am sorry. . . .'

It seemed pointless to argue. Now and again, however, Iori caught a glimpse of a mysterious light in the priest's eyes; but his bearing remained unaltered. Of one thing the youth was sure: the monk was mocking him. And to crown it all: Master Yamawaki and artifice! But even if that were so, it was not his present concern. The duel was the only important thing: he must break this insulting monk.

'You will agree without further argument!'

'No, a priest does not take hold of a spear!'

'Do you refuse?'

'How could I withstand an opponent like yourself?'

Iori could no longer contain himself: 'If you will not agree, I shall keep you here until you do.'

Without taking the slightest notice of Iori's outburst, Tesshin replied in the same gay manner: 'You intend to keep me here if I do not accept your challenge?'

'That is just what I intend.'

'Then I accept it.'

This answer took Iori completely by surprise and he could only stammer: 'What, you accept?'

If this is how it is going to turn out, his hasty outburst was no mistake, Iori thought, as he said:

'Thank you, Master. Forgive me for being annoyed and dis-respectful to you. But now let us get ready straight away.'

To this Tesshin replied: 'One moment. I accept your challenge. But I would like to warn you not to fight this duel.'

73

This, too! Tesshin had not dropped his gay manner, but he was no longer smiling; his eyes were flashing; his whole demeanour had changed.

Iori cried enraged: 'What! I am to give up the duel? How strange. And might I enquire why?'

'Because the result is already clear; why fight as well?' All of a sudden his tone had become sharp and his words rough.

'The result clear?'

'You are no opponent for me.'

Iori was speechless with rage. The atmosphere was tense to bursting point, but Tesshin betrayed no emotion.

'If you wish to know the truth: even your Master Gen-no-ju cannot avail against me. I can estimate the ability of his pupil without having to fence with him first. How can you hope to vanquish me when even your master cannot do so?' He broke into a loud laugh, 'Ha, Ha, Ha. . . .'

First accepted, then refused, finally made a mock of—Iori became red and white by turns.

Up to this he saw Tesshin as a priest who wished to humiliate him; now he had changed. The strange flashing of his eyes—the spirit emanating from him; he must be on his guard. Iori was beside himself. 'What impertinence! Stand up and make yourself ready!' He gesticulated with rage. . . .

'Iori, it is senseless to try to contend with you.'

'Get up, I say!'

Iori reached over him for one of the spears which lay at hand.

'Wait, one moment,' said the priest.

'. . . ?'

'A wooden spear? No, take a real spear and attack me.'

'With a sharp spear?'

'Yes.'

So much the better, Iori thought to himself as he replied: 'This is just what I wish.'

He went to fetch the spear. When he returned, he was wearing a belt, a mask, and all the other usual protective clothes, and was carrying two spears under his arm. But the priest was not to be found. He searched the garden rapidly and found him sitting in the grass, in the same strange posture as in the house.

The autumn sun was sinking fast and throwing long shadows over the shrubs and the lake.

Iori was still beside himself with rage and approached Tesshin, throwing the two spears at his feet.

'Choose one of them!' he said.

'I do not need a weapon in order to fight with one such as yourself,' replied Tesshin, not deigning to glance at the spears.

His face twitching and deadly pale, Iori hissed: 'Wretch!' Any further reply seemed pointless; and so he seized hold of one of the spears, threw back his mask and shouted: 'Here I come!'

The spearhead flashed, catching the last rays of the sun.

Tesshin rose without a word, and relieving himself of his upper garment with a rapid gesture, stood there, naked to his waist. . . . For a moment Iori was at a complete loss; his whole body shivered; then he recovered himself and advanced. 'Hai!' he shouted. But his voice sounded hollow. Only then did Tesshin turn towards him and look at him with eyes wide open. His head swinging to and fro, rolling, rocking, and his arms drawn in, he advanced slowly on Iori. A weird step like the dance of an octopus with one hundred tentacles. Iori could not find any position, not even the smallest point which would give him the advantage; not even the tiniest hole imaginable was exposed.

Iori was completely overpowered; there was but one thing for him to do: to retreat, step by step, one after another, in exactly the same rhythm as Tesshin was advancing. He felt as though he were being choked. His spearhead trembled; a cold sweat broke out all over him, those eyes—those eyes—the trembling spearhead began to jerk up and down. Iori could bear it no longer—he must scream—admit his defeat—but his voice failed him.

The evening shadows grew longer; already they were covering the whole garden and gradually beginning to ascend towards the sky.

Iori felt like a puppet being pushed in all directions.

Already he was approaching the pond in his retreat, he began to lose consciousness and the dancing octopus became blurred.

75

'Iori! throw your spear away!' came a voice from somewhere, the voice of his father. His spear seemed to fall of its own accord from his hand. He fell on his knees, his hands on the ground in front of him, and he could only stammer: 'I am utterly defeated.'

Iori's father bowed politely to Tesshin and said: 'I do not know who you are, but my son is obviously no opponent for you. Allow me to thank you, in his name, for teaching him the lesson his presumption deserved.'

Tesshin drew on his garment again and answered:

'My name is Tesshin, I am a hermit from the temple precincts of the Genkuji temple in Asakusa. Forgive me for the spectacle. With a little more attention to exercise Iori will become an excellent spearsman. Ha, Ha, Ha. . . .'

.   .   .   .   .

'Master.'

The next day, Iori, still pale from his encounter with Tesshin, knelt in front of Gen-no-ju and bowed deeply.

'O Master, your all-perceiving wisdom . . . yesterday Tesshin vanquished me utterly.'

Gen-no-ju closed his eyes slightly and said: 'So he vanquished you?'

'Yes, my skill is too poor to match one such as he.'

'Hm, it is ten years now since he became a hermit, but his skill seems undiminished. . . .'

'Master, who is this Tesshin?'

'Tesshin?' Gen-no-ju looked into the distance. 'Tesshin was one of my pupils for about ten years, when I had first begun to teach.'

'But, Master, why is such a great spearsman as he a solitary monk?'

'You see, Iori, it happened in this way. Like you, he had a natural flair. He had unusual skill, Iori. But he had no control over his feelings. He had a disagreement with an older pupil over some trifle; he challenged him to a duel and ran him through the body with a wooden spear.'

'. . . ?'

76

'He was filled with remorse and retired into solitude. We write to each other from time to time. He seems to have regained control over himself to some degree.'

Iori nodded to himself and said:

'Master, Tesshin said . . .' and then he related the details of Tesshin's behaviour before the duel, even telling of how he said that the master Gen-no-ju was no match for him. 'Why did he say a thing like that?' he asked.

Gen-no-ju's white beard was like a wave, as he threw back his head and laughed. 'Did he say that again? He is a fool! Twice I have sent pupils of mine to challenge him and twice he said the same thing.'

'. . . ?'

'Iori—the very fact that you could let yourself get annoyed at his words shows that your feelings are not yet disciplined. And so you fell straight into his trap. You have not yet got proper control over yourself.'

The master's words sank deep into Iori's soul.

'Discipline is not concerned with skill nor form alone. How often have I told you that? That is the whole point. In your outward bearing you have achieved a marked degree of discipline. But I felt that you still lacked sufficient self-control, the great discipline of the emotions. That is why I did not let you contend with me yet.'

'Yes, Master. . . .' Iori's heart overflowed as he now understood his master's inimitable goodness.

'I am getting old, Iori. My strength is leaving me. You only saw my physical strength diminishing, only the visible sign of my age. And so you became impatient. True—there is a limit to visible strength . . . but to the others, Iori? As long as you can be ensnared by what meets the eye, you still have a good way to go. Do you understand what I mean?'

Iori was deeply moved and his voice shook as he replied:

'Yes, yes—it is only now that I begin to really grasp your teaching.'

'Hm, Iori, that is right.' And after a short pause he added: 'Soon, yes, soon enough you may contend with me.'

77

'Thank you, Master, but I feel I am far from being ready yet.'
Once more Gen-no-ju's eyes were lit up in a kind, soft smile.

'No, no, Iori, once you have understood this, it is sufficient.
Let us meet soon.' And the master laughed contentedly.

Iori turned to one side; he felt that something new and good
had just been born in him—he went into the garden. His soul and
his heart were utterly pure. He struggled against the tears which
were just beginning to flow from his eyes.

The morning dew on the blossoms and the grasses at the edge
of the pool glistened in the rays of the rising sun.

II

The Identity of Ken-Zen

Expounded by Reibun Yuki in the spirit of the Zen priest Takuan[3]

The *Ken* or sword is one of the three sacred heirlooms of the Imperial House of Japan. The essence of the *kendo* (the way of the sword) consists in attaining to an understanding of its sacred meaning. It was Takuan, the Zen Master, who set out to explain the *kendo* from the point of view of Zen, at the beginning of the Edo era. This was a time when the true spirit of the *kendo* had become confused and was widely misunderstood.

.   .   .   .   .

Takuan's real aim was to explain why so many *kenkaku* (swordsmen) were unable to gain any knowledge of the true nature of *Ken*. Takuan attributed this to men being in the grip of the selfish desires of their ego, whereas in actual fact *kendo* is but a discipline by which man frees himself from the dominance of his own ego. Under the influence of a warlike age, *kendo* had become a matter of brute force and its true spirit accordingly misunderstood. It was Takuan's merit to have brought the soul of the sword to light once more.

.   .   .   .   .

The basic facet of his thought was: '*Ken* and Zen are one and the same.' What is the meaning of this? Some people try to interpret this on the grounds of 'common sense', expressing it something like this:

79

'The *Kendo* (Way of the Sword) and the *Zendo* (Way of Zen) have much in common.'

Only a beginner would think like that. The real meaning of their identity is quite different. A person who really understands *Ken* sees not only Zen but also the great law of heaven and earth and the whole universe as nothing but *kendo*; conversely, *Ken* and the phenomenal world are but the movements of the waves on the ocean of Zen. To express it still more forcibly, we can say that the identity of *Ken* and Zen is a plane on which neither of them exist any more, but where we can find nothing in the entire universe which is not *Ken* and not Zen. In the Obaku sect, the most rigorous of the Rinzai-Zen, there is the merciless *Sanzyubo* or thirty strokes of the stick, which an initiate in the *Zazen* exercise receives from time to time at the hands of the supervising priest, as an admonishment or to punish him. This, to a *Ken*-man, who has perceived its meaning, is none other than *Ken* descending like lightning from heaven on the head of an opponent. The *Sanzyubo* is also to be found in the *Kendojo* or place of exercise for the disciples of the sword. A Zen-man who has reached a similar level sees this speedy form of defeat in the *Dojo* (training place for the disciples of the sword) and regards it in the same way as he does the *Sanzyubo*, which can be the occasion of the 'Awakening' (*Satori*).

. . . . .

When a *kenkaku*, while fencing, becomes permeated and tense with the 'spirit', so that he dwells or rests where dwelling no longer exists (*muju*), he then becomes invulnerable so that the smallest possible hair or even the thrust of a Zen master can find no unprotected spot on his body. In other words it depends on whether the mind is recollected or distracted for the 'spirit' to be fully present or completely absent and the *kenkaku* vanquished or victorious. Therefore the right ability of the *kendo* is not concerned with aiming at one's opponent but with forging one's own spirit. In the last analysis what my opponent is depends on the degree of perfection of my own spirit: it is through this alone that a person determines what his opponent is.

. . . . .

In Zen or *kendo* we say of drinking tea or eating meals that, properly understood, they are nothing but Zen or that everyday habits such as walking or standing, sitting or lying, are nothing but *Ken*. Similarly we cannot say that *Ken* or Zen is something definite or special in itself. Everything is fundamentally *Ken*-Zen. If this is accepted, we can say equally well that *Ken* and Zen are non-existent or that the essence of *Ken* and Zen is contained in the very fact that everything is simply *Ken* and Zen. In other words only when a man has got over the so-called *Ken* and Zen can he comprehend true *Ken* and true Zen. For the same reason he can only claim to have a true grasp of the *kendo* and *kendo* when he discovers the real *dojo* everywhere in daily life and not only in connection with specific training centres. The same attitude regards a *zendo* with unfeigned contempt whose highest achievement is mere skill in fencing.

. . . . .

Zen culminates in an attitude of mind which stands the test of everyday life. Similarly the *Kendo* proves itself in the way a man conducts his daily life. Day and night are tense and filled with the spirit, that is, a right attitude of mind. A life such as this is one in which man has relinquished his own small ego, letting it be absorbed in the supreme Self and die for the sake of Justice. To see the *Kendo* as the art of the thrust and the parry is to miss the meaning of the great masters entirely and to desecrate *Ken*. That is the same as thinking of Zen as a sort of exercise in sitting.

. . . . .

Takuan declares at the beginning of the Taiaki: 'The art of fencing is never concerned with victory or defeat.'

What is the meaning of this? The saying is to be found in Miyamato Musashi[4] *Banri ikku*, i.e. 'one leads to ten thousand'. Ten thousand, that means ten thousand laws, in fact the whole complex of laws. Miyamato Musashi felt that this saying contained the secret of every art of fighting. If you speak of *ikku* in connection with *banri*, *Ku* then means emptiness in general and *ikku* signifies one particular void: within Buddhism this is more or less the same as '*Muga*' or 'egolessness', which is the stage reached by those who have received the supreme enlightenment and whose Ego-self has been entirely eliminated. The saying *banri ikku* used in connection with the art of conflict means therefore that only a man who has reached the stage of the enlightened one can contend in the right manner, using a thousand different turns and counter-attacks, uninhibited and faultless.

• • •

The Truth contained in the phrase *banri ikku* is only revealed when an individual person or thing, while preserving its own individual character, dismisses its lesser self and becomes assumed into the greater or 'self-less self'. Seen from above every object in the world is an inevitable part of the whole. If all objects were conscious of this fact and each of its basic significance and tension they would be able to reveal fully and rightly their individuality. Negating their little ego and so attaining to perfect selflessness, they would be infused with the universal force which embraces and permeates all individuality. This is the meaning of the phrase *banri ikku* and of the other one *bambutsu wa ittari nari* which says that all things in the world are basically one in essence—one body.

• • •

In the consciousness that all things are essentially one body the 'other' can be equated with oneself and oneself with the 'other' (or opponent). *Kendo* aims at bringing us to the level of such consciousness.

• • •

Common sense regards the art of conflict as one in which a contest against an enemy must be decided by means of position and

82

counter-position. But Takuan places at the head of his remarks the assertion that the art of conflict is unconcerned with victory or defeat, advancing or retreating, with strength or weakness. Not only the layman but the tried warrior is struck by this remark as though a flash of lightning had appeared in a clear sky. . . . Takuan explains his own phrase in the following words: 'a man should vanquish without moving a step from the spot where he is standing, neither forward nor backward'. This phrase contains the secret of the art of conflict and more than that—the secret of the conduct of all human affairs.

.　　　.　　　.　　　.　　　.

How can one conquer without fighting? Must we not learn the correct method of fighting if we are to gain a victory? True, but if we let our thoughts be misled by the word 'Method', we will be coaxed into mere fighting even against our own will. To regard 'method' as artifice and intrigue is to be led into 'mere' fighting. Anyone who devises the latter does so from an attitude bound in by the antithesis of 'the ego' and 'the counter-ego'. From such a viewpoint victory without having to contend is the very last thing to hope for and the only tangible result is a state which alternates between victory, if one's own artifices succeed, and defeat when those of the enemy succeed. 'In that case,' as a traditional remark of Sekiun on the *kendo* declares, 'a man will sometimes conquer one weaker than he, at others be conquered by one stronger, or at another perish against an equal. But a decisive result is un-attainable.' The secret of victory without conflict is never to be found in artifices or devious practices. In accordance with what has been said above, one must break through to the world where all things are essentially of one body. But let us hear what Master Takuan himself has to say of it.

Victory without contending—how can this be achieved? Takuan replies: 'It comes the moment the stage is reached when the enemy no longer sees me nor I the enemy, when heaven and earth are as yet undivided and light and shade are one, before *In* and *Yo* (Yin and Yang) reveal themselves.' Takuan explains the phrase: the enemy does not see me nor I the enemy in the following manner: 'I' in this context is synonymous with the personal ego (*ninga*). Everyone knows his own personal ego but few are aware of the true 'I' or *shinga*. The phrase therefore means that because I am not confronted with my own personal ego, I take no notice of the stratagems of the enemy's ego either. That does not preclude my having the enemy before my eyes and seeing him. To see him and not to see him, that is the wonder of it, that is the heart of the matter!

    .   .   .   .   .

The true self has existed from before the separation of heaven and earth, and before the individual was conceived by his parents. This self is alive within me, in others, in birds, quadrupeds, in plants and trees, in everything. It is the Buddhatwa or the Buddha nature of everything. It is a self which possesses neither shadow nor form, life or death. It can never be seen with the naked eye. Only the enlightened can perceive it. Anyone who has seen it is called 'one awakened to become Buddha by having discovered the Buddha nature'.

Sakyamuni once attained the Awakening after six years of hard-exercise on the mountain of Setzusan. That was the self-revelation (*Satori*) of the true self. How could an ordinary man attain to such an enlightenment in three to five years without the aid of faith? Buddhist initiates must therefore practise the most rigorous exercises for ten or even twenty years, persevering unceasingly from morning till night, in their efforts to realize the great power of faith. They exercise under priests of great virtue, sparing no pains of life or limb to get to the root of the doctrine, as eager in their efforts as a parent seeking a lost child. Perhaps one day they will reach the utmost limits of learning and as it were without an effort, attain the great enlightenment.

    .   .   .   .   .

Ogasawara Genshin, one of the disciples of the Kamiizumi Isenokamis, had some three thousand disciples. The first of these was a master called Hariya Sekiun. There is a book by him *Kempo Sekiun Sensei Soden* (Traditional aspects of the Kempo art of the Kendo) by Master Sekiun, which passes on his teaching to posterity. The master differentiates between the *kempo* of man's animal nature and that of his true human nature; he shows that the latter is the genuine image of the sword and the former mere illusion and error: the attitude in which *kempo* is the means enabling a strong man to defeat a weaker is derived entirely from our animal nature. The *kendo* derived from our true human nature, however, is the art of revealing the Buddha nature in man.

.   .   .   .   .

Describing Sekiun's views on the *kendo* in the words of Takuan, we may say that it is a question of the difference between the sword of the 'personal' ego and that of the 'true' ego. The personal ego, the one perceived by common sense, is always 'engaged' and self-seeking; it is always concerned with preserving its own 'status' and is partnered with someone of an opposing 'status'. A person who relies on this ego might at first find some things in common with another person. Sooner or later, however, he will come into conflict with him, because it is the nature of the personal ego to be opposed to someone else. He will eventually become the victim of his animal nature in order to survive. This is all true also of the *kendo*. When individuals fence with each other on the basis of their own personal ego, their conflict is a wretched one, since it is merely between strength—as far as physical strength, stratagems, and tricks are concerned—and weakness. If a man's adherence to his personal ego should correspond to the image of the universe and to the true life he would then be bound to act accordingly, no matter how hateful and wretched it was. But it is not so. The true image of life is only evoked in a mind which has banished its personal ego and let the real self come to light.

The sword of the personal, 'engaged' self must finally disappear into the realm of the beasts and the *Asura* (devils of conflict). This is simply because 'I' see the 'enemy' and the 'enemy' me, each persisting in its obstinate antagonism so as to engulf and destroy

85

the other. According to Takuan the true nature of the sword is quite the reverse of this attitude. This is the sense of the phrase: 'I do not see the enemy, nor he me.' It is only on the discovery of the genuine self overcoming the personal self that the true sword is revealed. As the proverb has it: 'Brigands in the forest are easily overthrown, but not so the brigand within us.' In *kendo*, too, the real enemy is not without but within. Once we are able to destroy him, that is, our personal self, then every external enemy will vanish of its own accord. In other words the elimination of the one is conditional on the revelation of the other. Takuan therefore says: 'It is necessary to have always the "One" before our eyes; in It, heaven and earth are as yet undivided, in *In* (*yin*) and *Yo* (*yang*) unrevealed. Man should learn to look straight into the heart of things and not be deflected by the discriminating and conceptual character of the surface.'

.   .   .   .   .

The true ego can never be revealed by the way of the intellect or the reason. When Takuan refers to 'the utmost bounds of all comprehensible Buddhist teaching', he means that all depends on man's persevering to the extreme limits of his power. It is only in this way that the illusory personal self can be torn apart and man at last can calmly forge the sword three *shakus* in length while hanging on the edge of the cliff, 'suspended between life and death'. A man who has exhausted himself for twenty or thirty years in unbroken endeavour may now be struck, as it were, by a thunderbolt in the sense of a vision of himself and his opponent as basically one, i.e. '*Not-Two*'. To 'forge' the sword is to forge oneself. To follow the way of the sword is to form one's inner self. Everything pays homage to the truly great and bows before the glory of its inherent dignity. To conquer without fighting means to bend others through the power of one's own virtue. This is the meaning of the 'true and wondrous sword'.

.   .   .   .   .

A man who gains possession of the 'true and wondrous sword' has the power to restore to life and to take it away. With this power,

86

he can conquer without fighting. Takuan expresses it in the following words: 'The master does not kill with the sword, he gives life with it. What must be killed, he kills and he gives life to what must be given life.' In the former, the *samadhi* of killing, in the latter, the *samadhi* of giving life.

Takuan expounds the phrase: 'the master does not kill with the sword' in this way: 'Even when the master does not "kill" with the sword his adversary is so terrified by the sight of Truth, which the master incorporates, that he becomes as if dead, nor can he find any vulnerable spot on the master.' The phrase 'he brings to life with it' is explained in the following manner: 'The master plays with his adversary, letting him carry out his plan of attack, and watches him calmly without killing; thus he brings the latter to himself. Thus he is free to kill or give life as he chooses.' The adept is familiar with this 'stage of the sword', where the sword is no longer synonymous with (external) killing, but is instead a life-giving art. The sword of a man governed by his ego cannot do this, even if he wishes it. In his hands it is involuntarily changed to an instrument of death. Thus it never depends on the actual sword itself: it depends on the man who is wielding it.

.   .   .   .   .

The sword of the personal ego belongs to an 'animal-like' soul, which sets enemies against itself. It is a part of the world of each against all in the struggle for existence. This is not only true of the world of the 'sword' in the narrower sense of the word. All relations between people for personal advantage point to the former or 'death-bringing' sword. One man cannot gain an advantage without harming the rest. Even if the principle of 'the common good before the individual' is set up, everything remains as it was unless the souls of the individuals themselves are changed. Buddhism speaks of the exercise in the footsteps of Buddha as *ichadaiji-innen* which means: 'the most significant cause and occasion of all.' This exercise means conquering one's personal desires and, in a world of selfish ambition, elevating oneself to the plane of truth and preserving it.

.   .   .   .   .

ichidaiji-innen is at once the life-giving sword and the sword which brings death, in the special sense where these are identical. As long as a person looks on them as two entities contradicting each other, he is far removed from the 'stage of the sword' in Takuan's sense. The sword of the master inflicts death on his adversary solely through his indwelling power. This power, given him by the true living self, annihilates the mere personal ego of the adversary. At the same time however the latter feels his own true self affected, just as everyone who comes into contact with a great man is stimulated to improve himself. The sword of the dexterous intriguer fails him when encountered by that of the master. It is forced to capitulate and the defeated realizes that his superficial art is of no avail and he must now strive to attain the other sword. In this way is the sword of death transformed into the sword of life. It arouses men to 'forge' their own self. The death-bringing sword of the master is the destruction of injustice and herald of justice.

.   .   .   .   .

There is a qualitative difference between doing something in the spirit of the personal, and doing it in the spirit of the genuine self. The one is artificially predetermined, the latter a natural out-flowing. There are therefore two types of action in the pursuit of the *kendo*; one is guided by human consciousness, while the other is direct and comes into being naturally without the air of con-sciousness. The latter has something in common with the work-ing of the universe. In the case of religious salvation the same difference exists. There is something artificial in a man racking his brains to find some way to be saved. How different the gradual progression of the believer who is seized by ecstasy at the sight of the Almighty! True action is action without acting (*musa*).

Yet this is not saying that action is non-existent. *Musa*, accord-ing to Takuan, 'is like a man who in his daily acts, has reached a stage beyond "doing anything"'. This 'doing nothing' is, if rightly understood, Supreme Acting, not on the sense of conscious progression, but an act transformed into a direct working of

88

natural laws. It is absolute action. It is a perfect mode of action, completely natural and as such not action at all—if we regard the latter as being synonymous with strain and effort. We could differentiate between inhibited action and uninhibited action: on the one hand those who are ruled by their past life, on the other those who can transcend their pást at any given moment. The actions of the latter are unselfconscious and they can live each moment fully. When the personal ego vanishes, time loses its grip: the true self has been won and men are beyond 'time'— and therefore fully present in each moment.

.   .   .   .   .

People are wont to speak of the necessity of a new order of things. Men in the grip of their personal ego and of time adhering to it, can only give birth to an 'old' order. A new order is, correctly speaking, one which is renewed hourly: only here can uninhibited action exist. This type of action is simply non-existent for one who is in bondage to time. He sees nothing as it really is, because he looks at it through the glass of his ego. This is the meaning of the Zen saying: *Zuisho ni shu to naru.* (Let a man be lord wherever he is, according to the place.) Takuan explains this by saying: 'Put a mirror down somewhere. Everything that is in front of it is reflected in it, exactly as it appears. The mirror has no consciousness, is unable to differentiate, therefore it reflects things exactly as they are. The same is the case with a master in the art of conflict. He is open to the pure mirror of his soul and it is unclouded by any trace of the consciousness which separates and distinguishes one thing from another, distinguishing between good and evil. Yet his mirrorlike soul is not blind to "this" and "that", to "good" and "evil"; he sees without being forced to see.' If the mirror of the soul is without consciousness, pure and free from the slightest trace of prejudice, then everything in heaven and on earth is reflected in it, just as it is. A man who possesses such a mirror is absolutely present in perfect command of the moment and the attitude of mind which is called for at that point. He is not beholden to 'this' or 'that', whether good or evil, to 'in' or 'out', 'up' or 'down', independent of any definite 'mode' of existence whatsoever. He and he alone can produce natural action, wonderful in that it can be subjected to every conceivable change, action without action, whether in the art of fencing or any of the arts of life, and containing in itself the wisdom of Buddha.

.   .   .   .   .

According to Takuan, one 'should be able to see good and evil without seeing them, be able to distinguish precisely without distinguishing them at all. One should be able to set one's foot on water as though it were earth and on the earth as though it were water. A man who can do this is peerless; yet he can only attain to this stage if he avails himself of every moment to advance in purity, whether he is walking, standing, sitting, lying, speaking or in silence, drinking tea or eating. He must strive unceasingly to keep sight of the true nature of things, endeavouring to comprehend it from every angle and so see into its very heart. And if with the passing of years it suddenly seems to him that a light has all at once appeared in the darkness, then he has reached some measure of understanding of the wisdom which no teacher can communicate; now he will be able to evince something of the miraculous activity which is contained in non-action. A master in the art of conflict who possesses such a mirror in his soul is free from every trace of the consciousness which divides and distinguishes. He sees everything without "seeing" it.'

.   .   .   .   .

To understand the wisdom which no master can communicate and reveal the wondrous activity of passiveness is what Takuan means by the word: *taia* or the 'sword of wonder'. According to him, a man who acts in this manner at all times has raised himself above the bounds of the commonplace without ever having crossed them. This is *taia*, the 'most excellent sword', potentially present in every individual. It is not until its full clarity is revealed that the very devil of heaven trembles before him. To omit to do it from the obscurity of one's own ego is to give oneself over to the basest of creatures.

The sword of wonder is innate in all of us; it is the mark of our perfection, bestowed on us by heaven from the beginning. Yet we are unaware that our nature has been enriched by such a jewel, we search in vain and let ourselves become dependent on others; we hide the jewel in the depths of our soul and become the victim of life's deceit in its basest creatures.

·　　·　　·　　·　　·

The 'artifices' promulgated in *kendo* are essentially lifeless. In order to become living beings and to develop their own powers, these must be first transformed so as to become part of the 'Supreme art'. The latter may be stimulated by 'external' instruction, but it is already present in the essential being. In fact no master can 'communicate' this art, for each man must recognize it in himself, quite apart from the master's teaching. *Kendo* is an art of the *kogebetsuden* (external specific teaching, communicated to each man individually) and of the *mushidokugo* (recognized by the individual without a teacher).

·　·　　·　　·　　·　　·

The true sword disposes over life and death in a free and miraculous manner, destroying wrong and revealing right. Once a man becomes aware of this sword in himself he sees his own small self-seeking ego decay and disappear. The innate true self appears of its own accord. The 'landscape of the soul' is revealed to him, which otherwise is only visible when the dignity and virtue of a master touches him, encouraging him to discover his true nature. But what happens when masters cross swords with each other? Takuan has the following words on such a 'landscape':

'When one *jozu* (adept) crosses the point of his sword with another, and no longer thinks in terms of victory or defeat, we are reminded of the tradition of how Kasho Bodhisattva smiled when Buddha held a flower between his fingers as he preached.'

There is a deep significance in this comparison between the swords of the two masters meeting and Kasho's smiling as Buddha turned a flower between his fingers without a word. This was the event concerned: When Lord Sakyamuni stood on the Reishu mountain and, without a word, held out a flowering branch to the crowd in front of him, no one was able to understand what he meant. Everyone remained still; none spoke nor knew what to do. Only Kasho understood what the master meant and he smiled. Buddha was filled with joy that his meaning had reached Kasho, for it could not be communicated in words nor in any definite 'teaching', only directly, from one soul to another. Thus, according to Takuan, the true nature of an encounter between two masters must remain incomprehensible to the ordinary man. Only a master could fathom it, from heart to heart. What takes place in such a meeting, and what its significance is, defies description. It must remain hidden from all except those who have themselves, through long exercise, become masters. Their world can only be faintly imagined by less advanced adepts.

.   .   .   .   .

On the towels which are distributed to the members of the *kendo* department of the University of Tokyo stands the motto: 'Play on the "way".' The characters are from the hand of the master Kinoshita. He was still alive and a master of the *kendo* when I was a student of the *kendo* department. The phrase has a meaning similar to that of Takuan in his reminder of Kasho's smile as the mark of an encounter of two masters. Miyamato Musashi, the supreme master of the sword, called himself Niten-Doraku, literally 'Lover in two heavens'. The word *doraku* means 'pleasure on the way' and undoubtedly indicates his frame of mind as a master. This stage of 'playing on the way', is also known in Buddhism as *horaku* (pleasure in Dharma) or *yugesammai* (*samadhi* of the game). The art of the master lies beyond intent and will, far removed from pedantic effort. It is a natural pleasure. Thus the crossing of their rapiers is no longer a conflict. Two individuals have become 'one' within one realm which has absorbed them both. Two individuals stand face to face, strictly speaking they are '*Not-Two*', for here is no 'self' and no 'other'. (*Jita-funi* = 'self-other: not-two'.) The two masters are as two modes of the same being, an image of supreme truth which has existed unchanged from all times in the *samadhi* of its play. That is how they show the stage of natural *dharma* pleasure. Truth in its visible expression and in enjoyment of itself is the sphere of movement of the masters when they cross swords.

.   .   .   .   .

The initiates strive towards mastery and even at this stage should have the taste for 'play on the way', pleasure in the *dharma*, the *samadhi* of playing. They must, of course, strive with all their power and even then they have to overcome temptation to relax; they become tired or even feel a sense of repulsion against the whole thing. As long as it is solely application which keeps them on their chosen path, they have obviously not yet reached an understanding of the 'way'; they are still at the very beginning stages. If they become one with the way, then their efforts are joined with real pleasure in the way itself, and this can be interpreted as the promise of great achievement. If the way becomes inner necessity, then mastery has been reached and all is *horaka*.

.   .   .   .   .

The ordinary individual has no feeling for what is outside common sense. To him ordinary man who is clever is already exceptional, although in actual fact this cleverness of ordinary people never crosses the bounds of the commonplace. Takuan declares the difference to be as follows:

'Anyone who has a clear concept of three objects although he has been shown but one, or who can tell the number of coins in a heap at a glance, he is clever above the average. But he who possesses "this thing", (*Satori*, that is, the Awakening) is able to cut anything into three pieces without having it shown to him and his then being able to form a concept of three objects. It is easier still for such a man to dispose of an opponent. He does not even show the point of his sword. He acts more speedily than lightning, with such speed, in fact, that the tempest cannot overtake him.'

Miyamato Musashi relates the following story:

'I have dedicated myself to the sword from my youth. When I was thirteen years of age, I won my first combat, overcoming one who was a professional in his art, whose name was Kihei Arima, from the Shinto school. At the age of sixteen I vanquished a fine fencer by the name of Akiyama, from the province of Tajima. At twenty-one I went on to the capital and often used to fight there with recognized fencers, but I was never once beaten. In the provinces I later met fencers from every school and won over sixty combats without losing a single one. I was over thirty years of age when I looked back at these victories and discovered that none of them could be attributed to true mastery of the art. I did not know whether I unconsciously possessed an efficacy which was in accordance with the Supreme Way, revealing in itself the natural law of heaven, or whether I had been victorious through some defect in my opponents. So I continued to practise from morning till evening until I should become, as it were, part of Truth itself. When I finally began to correspond to the Supreme Way, I was fifty years of age.'

Like Musashi there were other renowned combatants who were not content to be victorious so long as victory was not an inner necessity. Who could be assured that Musashi, who in sixty combats had never been beaten, would be victorious in the seventieth? The goal of the fencer lies beyond ordinary supremacy; it is out of the realm of the commonplace. Musashi's words, 'When I finally began to correspond to the Supreme Way, I was fifty years of age,' refer to the 'extra-ordinary', i.e. to the stage of the enlightened one.

. . . . .

Takuan has explained in the following words the nature of the extra-ordinary sword: 'He who has reached this stage can at once divide anything into three parts, both before an object has been shown to him and before he has had time to form a concept of three distinct objects.' The image 'to be able to estimate the value of a heap of coins with the naked eye' refers to the ordinary sword. This is the sword of the sharply discriminating intellect, acting in accordance with some given proposition and always distinguishing between objects, whereas the extra-ordinary sword becomes effective without the agency of reason.

If we put a boy through his exercises in fencing, we are able to observe what he is aiming at and what his thoughts are, even before he actually starts to attack. We see in his face if he is going to strike our forearm, our face, or our body. This does not mean that we already possess the sword which 'can cut anything into three pieces straightaway'. Our understanding comes from the signs which he gives us. The stage of seeing without seeing, when signs are superfluous, is the stage of victory without combat. When we become as one without adversity, then we have attained this stage. Only when this is so are we enabled to understand our opponent without the aid of signs. Expressions such as 'Everything in the world is of one nature', the 'true ego', 'perfect self-lessness', 'effectivity without action', 'having power over life and death', etc., all refer to the same thing, to the highest stage of the sword *taia*. How can it be reached? Not through the agency of reason, but by inner activity and long exercise. The highest stage cannot be described in words nor expressed in laws or rules. It is Truth, and Truth exists outside rules or regulations, communicating itself naturally, only after long exercise. For supreme activity there are no rules any more.

III

The Tao of Technique

A text of the Zen Master of Archery, Kenran Umeji[5]

There is but one way to evoke Tao, one which defies description: 'from heart to heart'. There are many practical means of proving this way, which if they are practical in the right spirit, are altogether forms of realizing, Tao. There is the 'Tao of technique'. If technical perfection in any exercise (*gyo*) results in the right attitude, it is in itself a revelation of Tao. In the Tao of technique the latter becomes Tao, and Tao technique. Thus Tao = technique and technique = Tao.

In archery a man must die to his purer nature, the one which is free from all artificiality and deliberation, if he is to reach perfect enjoyment of Tao. He must learn how to control the admittance of Truth, flowing like an eternal spring. Finally he must be able to reveal Tao in his own attitude on the basis of true 'insight'. This way is a very easy and direct one. The most difficult thing is to let oneself die completely in the very act of shooting.

This 'dying completely' is not death such as one forces on oneself in a form of pointless agony of soul and body, arching and holding the bow in such a manner as to overtax one's strength. The correct manner of 'dying' gains freedom over life and death, by raising one above both, discovering one's true being and finally being absorbed in the Life which is beyond life and death. What matters is the death of that 'ego' which is in constant contradiction both to what is absolute and to what is relative.

To facilitate the death of his lower self, a man must exercise unceasingly and gradually acquire the right attitude. He must do this under the guidance of a master who himself possesses and evinces it. The first step is to achieve formal mastery over every single part of the act of shooting until he sees these as forming a certain 'figure'. The natural rhythm is then so much a part of him that no trace of tension or physical awkwardness remains. Secondly he must learn to free himself from the influence of the emotions and become as pure as a child. All at once, he realizes with his inner eye the 'figure' of the act of shooting quite apart from objective consciousness. Shooting as pure 'form', of which this figure is the reflection, appears of its own accord, effortless, without his having sought for it. The way to purity is a necessary prerequisite of the *Gyo-Tao* and can be attained in two ways: a man must learn to surmount intentional awareness and all emotional fluctuations. Only then can he perceive his innermost nature and hear the ear's own voice, that is, the voice of a creature in search of Tao. Or he can follow the path of objective intentional awareness to its limits and discover, in the very agony of his failure, the rhythm of eternal progression.

Anyone who is successful in either of these two ways has freed himself from the artificiality of 'making' an effort. Absolute purity is nothing but manifestation of Tao. In purity, Truth is realized. An ancient and holy man once declared: 'Purity or lack of it are synonymous with reaching or having failed to reach Tao. The only way to Tao is purity.'

In every exercise one must make all possible effort from the very outset to dispel impurity. What is impurity? Impure is whatever is based upon the ego-aspect, or caught in the grip of the ego. A man usually takes up an exercise in this attitude—ego-centred, that is self-willed, ambitious—and so he cannot free himself from the dualism of 'right' and 'wrong', 'good' and evil', being and non-being. He is confused, a prey to doubt and disbelief. As long as an ego-aspect as to the final goal is predominating, he cannot acquire the right disposition. Even if he should perceive and recognize the latter in himself, he is unable to prove it, despite his efforts. He is in the unenviable position of being caught in his ego-attitude unable to improve although he is conscious that his present state is wrong. He can never become part of Tao in this way; only the one, all-transforming change of heart can do this; it alone can purify him. Until this is effected, the way 'from heart to heart', is concealed from him. He is a man who is standing 'outside Tao'.

What is the sense of 'inside' or 'outside' Tao, as applied to an exercise? There are three classes of initiates: There are those who are quite outside Tao, striving to find it where it is never to be found. They are conscious of something wrong in their basic attitude and are convinced by the correctness of that of others, whom they endeavour to emulate. But in reality they are so much a prisoner of their wrong attitude that they have no real notion of what is right and wrong, although they appear to do so. Thus they cannot transform into the right attitude what they take to be the wrong one, and they are unable to get rid of the wrong attitude, even when they perceive the right one. So they never get away from the conflict of right and wrong, good and evil. They may chance on a proper disposition and become recollected and peaceful: for a moment they realize what they have found, but the old conflict soon reasserts itself. This is going astray in contradiction or 'dualistic confusion'. A person caught in its meshes is still outside Tao and the way 'from heart to heart' is still closed to him.

There are others who are already 'inside' Tao. If they continue their efforts in the right manner, they will not fail to come to where Tao is manifest. But at the beginning they will go astray in their own dwelling within Tao.

There are some within Tao who are really familiar with the true attitude and endeavour in the right manner to free themselves from the false one. Yet they have difficulty in actually establishing the former. Should they attain it through perpetual exercise, they suddenly stop moving and are not only unable to advance any further, they slip back into the old attitude without realizing it.

Each of these latter groups must eventually receive enlightenment, because neither gives up. In both cases, it is just a matter of 'going astray in their dwelling within Tao' or 'within appropriate recognition'. In reality this is not going astray at all. Here too, we find that 'giving and receiving from heart to heart'. Finally there is the stage where every thought, act, and demeanour in one's entire being is a revelation of Tao. This is the stage of mastery.

What we have been describing as persons outside Tao, is but the lowest stage in the pursuit of archery. It is the stage of actual learning, whereas in all the other stages there is something more besides. The pupil's efforts at shooting have given way to the act itself. (Here 'act' is not to be understood in the sense of the ego taking aim, but of the activity of Tao through the medium of shooting.) The training process is subject to the law of life. The way of progress in one's exercise leads from mastery of outward technique to the possession of 'actual' technique; from mastery of outward form to the evoking of Supreme Form which embraces all individual forms; from fulfilling outward rules to the fulfilling of the Supreme Law; from the particular path, to the Path. Progress is not merely a question of time. It depends entirely on 'where one's heart is', on the great transformation; all of a sudden a man can experience the 'Great Insight'. Thus the stage of 'perfect awareness' is not to be gained through systematic advance: it is a matter of sudden revelation.

Archery is one way of evoking Tao. It is one mode of the way. The way of attaining to Tao by the pursuit of archery, in the way of acquiring the right attitude in the very moment of shooting. To achieve this the individual must become pure and he must die. For only if his ego is dead, can he come to understand the meaning of 'technique = Tao' and can manifest Tao 'in the proper use of wisdom', thus establishing the insight which he has received. Tao is, at bottom, absolute purity. This is synonymous with the great Truth which embraces the universe as a whole. Essentially the heart of a Tao-man, that is, of a person who manifests and establishes Tao without any effort, and the heart of one who is still searching for Tao are both of them simply a mode of Great Purity, indeed they are Purity itself: the difference between them is merely that, in the case of the seeker it is as yet dim and undeveloped, whereas in the case of the enlightened one, purity reveals itself in its full light.

The relation between master and disciple is similar. What the master evokes naturally and what the disciple is striving to acquire, can coincide all of a sudden and quite unexpectedly, and something deepset in both is revealed: the heart of the master and the heart of the disciple are suddenly one. This is what is known as the 'way from heart to heart'—thus Tao can only be 'transmitted' to one who already 'possesses' it.

Masters and disciples scattered throughout the world, reflect for a moment whether you are inside or outside Tao!

Notes

1 A special monograph, *Hara, die Erdmitte des Menschen*, by the author, has been published by Otto Wilhelm Barth-Verlag, Munich-Planegg, 1956. 2nd edit. 1959. English edition, *Hara, the Centre of Personality*, by George Allen and Unwin, London.

2 The path of this exercise is a long and difficult one. Eugen Herrigel has discussed it in connection with archery. At this juncture I would like to recommend his work: *Zen und die Kunst des Bogenschiessens* (Otto Wilhelm Barth-Verlag, Munich-Planegg) most warmly. It is based on personal experience and is therefore a reliable and invaluable introduction to the purpose, method, and elements of this art. Engl. translation, *Zen in the Art of Archery*, by Pantheon Books Inc., New York.

3 1573–1645. The monograph of Reibun Yuki printed here reproduces a famous text—the *Taiaki*. It has been abridged for publication and a few non-essential sections omitted.

4 1582–1645. Famous master in the art of fencing and Zen painter.

5 Kenran Umeji, who taught me archery, is still alive today and well known as a Zen master and master of this art.

A detailed study of the problems connected with the 'cult of tranquillity' and the 'inner way' is to be found in other works by the same author.

1 *Im Zeichen der Grossen Erfahrung*. (Otto Wilhelm Barth-Verlag, Munich-Planegg. 2nd edition 1958.)

2 *Durchbruch zum Wesen*. (Max Niehans Verlag, Zürich. 2nd edition 1956.)

3 *Der Mensch im Spiegel der Hand*. (Otto Wilhelm Barth-Verlag, Munich-Planegg.)

4 *Erlebnis und Wandlung*. (Max Niehans Verlag, Zürich, 1956.)

INDEX